RELAUNCH MY LIFE

A guide to help you reconnect to your soul, redesign your future and rediscover the magic within.

JULIET LEVER

Copyright @ 2017 by Juliet Lever

Update: Revised Edition released in 2022.

ISBN: 978-064-6966-809

Editor: Bridget Ransome

www.julietlever.com

Prologue

5 years have passed since I wrote the book you are holding in your hands.

So much has evolved since then.

My business has evolved. My life has evolved. My views have evolved. This book helped me reach more people and make an impact beyond what I could have imagined and for that reason I have not revised the book considerably.

I have chosen to add this prologue because I wish to add a planted thought to these pages.

What I have realised 5 years on, is that we do not simply relaunch our lives once and then remain in a stagnant place.

Life is a constant process of evolving and relaunching new versions of ourselves.

And so this opening serves to gently encourage you that you don't need to do anything FOREVER. You will take steps forward and have new realisations and new insights and understandings. As the world changes and as you change.

And in 5 years you will look back on the decisions you made to relaunch your life today and be so grateful for your courage and commitment.

I trust that this book has reached you at the perfect time in your journey.

And I am blessed to have you read the messages within this book.

Enjoy the journey

xx
Juliet
June 2022

Welcome.

Before we start, I am curious to ask, how do you enjoy reading books?

Some people like reading books from start to finish.

Others prefer to open a book to whatever page calls to them and read a random section on a particular day.

I've even heard of people who read books from the end all the way back to the beginning.

What I love about the world today is that a book was once a static piece. It was something that you would finish and then curiously read the 'about me' section about the author, feeling they were a million miles away and not a part of your life.

Today, we have the unique ability to connect.

I invite you to **connect with me**, and take advantage of our modern day ability to interact and become a part of each other's journey.

Please, take the following two steps before reading any further:

1. Firstly, join my Private Facebook Group 'Relaunch My Life Community' to join myself and a group of like-minded people on a similar journey to you.

2. Visit www.julietlever.com and register for my resources which includes my **FREE 'Relaunch My Life in 30 days' Calendar in the 'Book' resources tab**. Each step in this calendar over 30 days will gently guide you to take one action each day that will inspire and help you to relaunch any areas of your life. Print this out as you read along. There is also a PDF download of all the activities in this book.

These two steps will help you to stay focused on your path to self-discovery in relaunching your life, and you will gain valuable support, knowing that you are not alone in your journey.

Let's get started...

Contents

Introduction

I need to tell you a secret.

The book you hold in your hand today almost died a slow and painful death in the presence of self-inflicted perfectionism and criticism.

There were endless drafts…

I cursed the damn thing day and night for not being 'perfect.'

I had romantic ideas about the process of 'writing my own book,' but the reality was most of this process involved all night writing sessions only to throw my work away and wearily start all over again the following day.

But despite the challenge, I persevered for two reasons:

The first reason was that a few months ago, I was told something profound.

I was told that the very thing that would hold me back from writing this book would be *the very thing that would ruin my life.*

Those words haunted me as I realised the combination of procrastination and perfectionism was hanging like a heavy weight over publishing this book.

Writing this book has been one of the most challenging processes I have ever endured. Not because it's hard to write words from my heart. But because it's hard to decide when it's ready! When is it 'good enough' to publish? *Whatever that means.*

The process I put myself through in writing this book makes me wonder how many beautiful and inspiring gifts perish in the presence of our own self-criticism?

Isn't it incredible how we criticise ourselves before the world even has a chance to criticise us!

In doing so, we rob the world of our talents before they've seen the light of day.

What magic does the world miss out on because we don't believe our story is inspiring enough, or our art-work beautiful enough, our voices strong enough?

I am curious to know, what hidden magic is lying dormant in you right now?

What gifts are you hiding from the world?

This is the second reason I persevered in writing this book.

I regularly ask myself 'how can I be of most service to this world?' Whilst writing this book, I have received the same message from within in response:

'Share your message. Inspire and empower people to feel safe to bring their hidden gifts and magic out into the world.'

In order to do this, throughout this book I will share my personal journey of transformation and how I relaunched my own life, and small stories of clients I have worked with.

Each chapter starts with a segment I share with you from my journey and then leads into helpful tips, a take away and an activity for you to reflect upon.

I share more of my journey to begin with, as the book progresses I gradually share with you more processes, activities and resources. These steps will help you no matter where you are on your life journey.

The reason I have written this book in this unique style is because I believe I am here to share my story to inspire you to live a life of your highest potential and a truly authentic life. And sometimes it's not the amount of information, *but rather the amount of inspiration and application* of information that can cause the biggest change.

I also believe that an inspiring story and unique perspective on the world can be a potent remedy to an under-nourished soul.

So, whether you are seeking a total relaunch of your life, your career, your home life or whether you are just curious about what else the world has to offer, I urge you to stay open to the messages within this book— because your intuition has led you to read this book.

And whilst some of the concepts are simple, it is simple concepts applied masterfully that have the capacity to make dramatic differences in changing any areas of our lives for the better.

I am also going to share with you everything I possibly can that you need in your journey right now, from my unique and honest perspective.

I will share tips on how to prepare for the adventure that awaits as you redesign your life, the five keys to fulfilment, how to exercise your dreaming muscles, how to deepen and listen to your intuition, how to reconnect to your soul, how to be your own psychic, how to calculate your daily survival rate in life and how to interpret the clues that get left in your life.

My intention for sharing these tools and concepts is to plant seeds of curiosity to inspire you to live your most fulfilling life, no matter what your current reality may be. This book is not to give you all the answers to life. It is to help give you clues on your quest and help you to find the answers within.

I want to help you seek out those gems deep inside you and bring your magic out into the world.

Whilst I don't have a Harvard degree nor decades of experience, I offer you the perspective of a brave and inspiring woman. A woman who, despite many warranted fears and obstacles, has transformed her own life and now is ready to share her story with the world.

This book is a gift to all of the soulful humans of this world who feel like there is more to this life than just earning money, performing thankless tasks and meeting sales targets or unrealistic deadlines.

I know that's not why you were born.

I know that if you are reading this book then you know, deep down that **you were born to serve a higher purpose.**

This book is designed to inspire and empower you to move forward towards your dreams and to feel hungry to find the answers your soul is seeking.

To help you find your own truth, and forge your own path.

And to bring your unique magic to the surface.

I look forward to walking alongside you on this journey.

xx

Juliet Lever

Gratitude

I would like to thank every single person I have ever met in my life, as each interaction has shaped me into the person I am today.

And, I would *especially* like to thank:

Mum and Dad, thank you for giving me an incredible life and magical childhood. For giving me a beautiful experience of a combination of spirituality, wisdom, free thinking and opportunity. This start at life gave an independent soul like me the chance to shine.

My beautiful sisters Eva and Rosie for encouraging me always. My brother Sam for being a wise soul beyond his years.

To all of my friends, clients, supporters and our students, you are all incredible and inspire me daily.

An enormous thank you goes to Paul. Thank you for holding my hand through so many of my life experiences these past few years and for making me believe in miracles. Thank you for loving me more than I knew was humanly possible, for your passion, ideas, fun every day and for making me laugh more than I ever have in my life. Thank you. Endlessly, thank you. I will never be able to fully express what sharing my life with you means to me. Thank you for turning my life upside down.

And finally to you, my reader - thank you for reading this book. Thank you for stepping up in the world and for getting to the place in your life where you are ready to receive this book's message. Thank you for choosing to live life fully, bravely and curiously.

CHAPTER 1

You Were Born For a Reason

'It is not ease that we crave, but meaning and purpose.'
– Kenentsu Takamori

'Is this it?'

'Is this all there is to my life?'

These are the questions that I asked myself back in 2013.

Before I became the woman I am today.

Today I am a successful Transformational Coach, Certified Yoga Instructor, an International NLP Trainer Teacher. I have a Bachelor of Metaphysics, Business and Finance Diplomas, Coaching, Trainer Certifications in Neuro-Linguistic Programming (NLP) and Time Line Therapy® Techniques, Heartmath™ and Hypnosis.

I have been interviewed on International Summits, Radio Shows, hugged Tony Robbins, featured in newspapers and am the host of the Podcast 'Relaunch My Life Radio' where I share 10 minute tips and have interviewed amazing teachers such as Dr John DeMartini.

I am in a deeply fulfilling relationship, live in a beautiful home in South Australia and make a difference in the world.

I am healthy and vibrant and feel a deep sense of inner peace about my life, my choices and my future.

And it wasn't until very recently that I realised— *I am the woman of my dreams!*

But back in 2013 my life was a very different reality.

I could have never dreamed the life I am living today was even possible.

Yes, my life wasn't always this way —

Even though there was nothing visibly wrong, back then, at the age of 26, I would often ask myself 'Is this all there is to my life?'

From the outside anyone looking in would have said that I had it all, and from the look of it, I suppose I did.

So why did I feel so empty?

I was successful.

I had a well paying job in the corporate world running a large sales team for a company that I felt was making a positive difference in the world.

I was married with a $10,000 diamond ring on my finger to prove it.

I had a brand new luxury car, with expensive smelling black leather seats, tinted windows and GPS.

I had a wardrobe full of expensive, beautiful clothes and an endless amount of hand-bags I hardly ever used.

I had lots of beautiful, supportive friends.

This was my life and it all seemed so perfect from the outside— so why was I so unhappy?

Underneath all of this external success, deep down inside of me I felt like something was missing.

I felt like I wasn't enough and over time that feeling manifested into a deep and debilitating daily battle with anxiety.

I worked extremely hard during the week, a true workaholic. I poured myself into my career and was rewarded for it with pay-rises and promotions.

However, it seemed that the more I achieved the worse I felt.

Due to my low self-esteem I often thought that I was paid too much for what I did. I sometimes felt like a fraud.

I gave a lot to my work, and worked my way up to managing a large national sales team. My team loved me and I prided myself on being a caring, inspiring and authentic leader. I enjoyed seeing my team succeed and shielded them from the pressure on my shoulders to grow and expand the company quickly. Every-time I received a bonus or a pay-rise I would feel a little more stressed because it felt like the pressure and expectation rose at the same time.

On the home front, my husband and I had been together since I was 16 years of age. He was eight years older than me when we met and had very set views on life. He wanted me to be happy, but the reality was that although we were supportive and encouraging of one another, my marriage was passionless. It felt like we were flatmates and I would often fall asleep sighing, feeling undesirable and wondering 'is this all there is? I'm only 26 years old, have I already had all the passion I am going to experience in this life?'

I had never been single in my adult life, so I sometimes would question what life would be like if I was single. It was a fascinating thought for me to ponder, especially when my girlfriends would share stories with me about their exciting love affairs and the different men they met.

I felt guilty for even entertaining such thoughts and I would call myself a 'bad wife.' I would scold the curious, imaginative side of myself for even thinking this way and in the process I learned to shut down those innocently curious parts of myself that were yearning for my attention.

So, I turned to chocolate for pleasure and to mask the guilt I felt for wanting more out of my life.

I would eat an entire block of chocolate in one sitting and feel slightly better. It was my way of finding pleasure amongst a numb existence. But the pleasure was always temporary.

By the age of 26, I had begun to experience such intense physical symptoms of anxiety, my heart would palpitate and I was in constant fight or flight mode.

It seemed no matter what I did I always felt anxious.

At the end of a long day or on the weekend I would reach for wine or vodka which would temporarily ease my state of mind.

My friendships were largely based on alcohol, not thinking twice about drinking 15 to 20 standard drinks on a Saturday night. It was normal. It's what all of my friends did. I didn't see anything wrong with it at the time, but looking back, I was bordering on becoming an alcoholic.

Yes, I was stuck in a rut. And it seemed like no matter how I tried to escape it, I just couldn't break away from it. And the worst part was I didn't know there was anything else possible for me in my life. I felt trapped and I couldn't see a different future for myself.

If only I could tell that Juliet what I know today...

I think the worst thing about being trapped was not even realising that I was. I honestly thought that I was doing everything right, and that's why I couldn't understand what was happening to me.

I would put on a positive face at work and try to mask what I was feeling, but I knew deep down inside that I was living a lie.

Looking back now, I can see that I had no idea how to change and the life I was living was all I really knew.

I felt so alone and afraid to take any chances on something new.

Until one day, I received a wake up call.

This arrived in the form of a conversation with a fun and quirky entrepreneurial man I met whilst on a business trip hosted by a marketing company.

We were chatting to one another on the back of a sailing boat off the coast of Port Lincoln in South Australia, as we were returning from a shark cage diving expedition they had funded for their executive clients.

It was a beautiful sunny day and the wind was in my hair. I was probably still running off of the adrenaline of sharing a cage with three other people whilst eight Great White sharks rammed the small cage. It was an experience I will never forget.

I had my arm up at my face as we spoke, partly to cover my eyes from the sun and partly to make sure my brand new designer sunglasses wouldn't fall off of my face, thanks to the choppy water!

I had been warned prior to the trip that expensive jewellery could fall off whilst diving, so I wasn't wearing my wedding ring. My curious mind wondered if he was being nice to me because he thought I was single...

Standing at the back of the sailing boat, the man asked me, smirking as he took a swig of his premium beer, 'So, Juliet ... tell me what you do outside of work?'

I paused… Too long…

I swallowed. My throat was dry.

I realised, all of a sudden I was *very uncomfortable* because I couldn't answer his question.

What do I do outside of work? I asked myself, angry for not being able to think of something to say.

If I had been honest I would have said 'Well, let's see … I get drunk on weekends. I stress about work on week-days and when I get home I eat chocolate and drink red wine! I feel like there is something wrong with my life ALL the time; my heart palpitates NON-STOP; I have no passion in my life and I desperately need help!'

After that realisation, I felt sick to my stomach. I stammered a reply that said something 'fluffy' like 'Oh, you know, I hang out with friends and go shopping.'

But from that moment on I became real with myself.

I finally admitted that something significant had to change in my life.

This was me— unhappy, unhealthy and disconnected back in 2012

****

Just like that conversation I had on the back of the boat that day, I believe that everything happens for a reason.

I also believe that you have found this book for a reason.

Trust that this guide is a clue on the quest of your life journey.

By reading on I assure you, you are on the right path. There are no coincidences in life.

In this book, you hold the key to whatever obstacle you are facing in your life. There may be light-bulb moments, there may be crazy parallels between your life and mine, or you may be feeling a similar way to one of my client's situations that I will share in these pages.

My intention in these chapters is to guide you to a place within yourself that might feel far away right now.

You see, if you are anything like I was a few years ago you have most likely realised by now that **external things just don't feel fulfilling anymore.**

Clothes, food, alcohol, any addiction, you know it's just not enough anymore.

It may feel like something is missing and no matter where you look, or what you try to do, you just can't find it 'out there.'

You know you need to look within.

Perhaps you are reading this book because you feel unfulfilled in your work life.

Perhaps you feel like there is something you could relaunch about your home life or enhance in your relationship.

Perhaps you are trying to heal an addiction or emotional imbalance or maybe you are curious about exploring more on your spiritual path.

Perhaps you have a dream that frightens you a little, but you are finally ready to start taking steps to bring that dream to life.

Maybe you feel like you've been on the merry go round of life long enough. Repeating the same job, the same experiences, the same comfort (or discomfort!) zones for as long as you can remember.

There is a part of you that knows you were born to serve a higher purpose than your current situation. To experience a life of love, passion and fulfilment.

This book has been written to support you on your path, the ups and the downs, and so you know that you are not alone in your journey of finding your most fulfilling life.

No matter how off track you feel your life path is, I want you to know that you're reading this book for a reason.

My Mum often says this to me when I tell her about my life these days:

'Met je neus in de boter vallen, Juliet.'

It is a Dutch saying which roughly translates to *'you always fall with your nose in the butter'* which means to be lucky in life, or that when something bad happens, something good happens afterwards.

I believe that it is possible for incredible things to happen to all of us, *if we allow ourselves to fall every once in a while.*

And trust me when I say, with the beauty of hindsight, that if something wasn't meant to be happening in your life, it wouldn't be happening.

Just like that conversation I had on the back of the boat, the day I had my wake up call.

Once I had that realisation, deep down I knew I was born to do more, to have more, to give more and to experience more.

And I know you were too.

You were born for a reason.

And when you find and follow that reason — you thrive.

So before you read any more of my journey and I guide you through this redesign stage of yours, take a moment to decide what your intention is for your life as you read on.

I promise you will get so much more from this book if you have an intention from the beginning.

It may be 'I want to explore my intuition,' or 'I want to change my career' or 'I want to start being more brave.'

Whatever it is, take some time to think about why you are reading this book out of the millions of books available to you, and I promise you it will profoundly impact your experience.

KEY TAKE-AWAYS

- You were born for a reason. When you find that reason, you thrive.
- If you're truly living life then it's natural to have highs and lows.
- I'm here to guide you through a time of change and awakening.

ACTION

What is your intention for reading this book?

CHAPTER 2

_____

_____

_____

Let Your Soul Sing

'There came a time when the risk to remain tight in the bud was more painful than the risk it took to blossom.' – Anaïs Nin

A few weeks after my wake up call, I was flying home solo from an interstate business trip.

I always feel so wonderful when I travel. I find that flying above the clouds gives you a different perspective on life.

A birds-eye view on all the problems 'down there.'

As the plane landed I had been listening to an Abraham Hicks audiobook and as suggested I began thinking of lists of anything and everything in my life I was grateful for.

I quickly reeled off a list in my mind.

I thought about how grateful I was for my friends and family, my brand new car, my health. I continued thinking about how grateful I was for my team at work, for my opportunities in life, for my job.

As I listed everything in my mind I felt something inside my heart bubble up and burst. Suddenly a rush of tears started streaming down my face.

The man sitting next to me reading a John Grisham thriller asked me if I was okay.

I replied back at him through the tears 'Yes! I'm just so happy that I'm crying! It feels incredible!'

He smiled uncomfortably, and said 'Oh that's okay then!' and awkwardly buried his nose straight back into the safety of his book.

I realised that **my tears of gratitude were in fact, tears of joy!**

I had NEVER cried because I was happy... ever before in my life.

Not on my wedding day.

Not when I bought my first car.

Not when I got my kitten.

This simple moment of presence, gratitude and joy in an airport was so overwhelming for me.

I felt high. Giddy. Alive. Free.

I felt a depth of emotional connection that I had never experienced before deep inside of me.

My vibration was high and I felt like life would never be the same again!

I drove home from the airport saying to myself 'I am so happy I am crying!' Over and over again!

It would have sounded so crazy, but I just started talking to myself and had a moment of clarity— a soul connection that I had never experienced before.

I said to myself:

'Oh wow, I get it now! I FINALLY understand why I have had anxiety! I understand why things have felt 'off' for me in my life!'

'I finally get it!

*My purpose in this life is to connect people to their souls and emotions and **to help them feel this way!***

That's why I have felt like something is missing — I'm not following my soul's purpose in life!

I want to help people connect to their souls and make a real difference in this world, not just make a company lots of money and live a soul-less existence!'

As I arrived home I flew through the front door and greeted my startled husband with my excited realisation 'My purpose is to connect people to their souls! I want to be a life coach and help people find their soul's purpose!' I blurted out.

And, to be expected – he was concerned.

In hindsight I realised that I sounded legitimately insane!

He tried to help calm me down and bring me back down to earth by being practical.

'Jules, you have a good job,' he said. 'You're successful. Everyone knows that life coaches don't make any money. You earn good money in your job! You need to chill out. What's happened to you?'

I muttered something ungraceful under my breath about him being a 'dream crusher' and went to unpack my suitcase in a huff.

But a seed had been planted in me.

And I wouldn't let it go.

Yes, after that day everything really started to change.

My soul had spoken to me for the first time in my adult life and I was determined to connect with it deeper and deeper each day.

****

You were born to live your happiest and most fulfilling life and everything you are experiencing is guiding you towards that.

So if you truly want to find where you are going, the first thing you need to do is find out where you are right now.

Why is that so important?

Your brain is completely different today than what it was yesterday due to new thoughts and feelings.

You have breathed air today that you've never breathed before so your lungs are entirely different.

Who you are in this exact moment in time today has never existed before.

Because of the experiences you have had today and the thoughts and feelings you are having right now reading this book, you are not the same person you were yesterday.

So, let's explore where you are at today.

Without over-thinking write down your answers to the following question:

In life, what things do you generally get curious or excited about?:

1. _____

2. _____

3. _____

4. _____

5. _____

For some of us it's animal rights, for others it's meditation, for some it's cooking or sport. It's different for us all! And if you struggled to answer the above section, that's okay, you can come back to these questions again any time.

It's important to note that the things that inspire and excite you can change over time (especially after life-changing experiences).

So start getting excited and curious, about what you are excited and curious about today!

Remember, *no one else knows what makes your soul sing, but you.*

****

Have you ever stopped to explore your soul beliefs?

What I am referring to is the part of you that isn't your brain, that isn't your body and that isn't just your chemical and hormonal responses.

The part of you that is eternal.

If we entertain the idea that you are an eternal being, then in this lifetime, why are you, experiencing life as you?

Consider this for a moment.

Out of all of the places in the world you are living, here you are in your city, in your country.

Out of all of the families you could have grown up in, you were born into yours.

Out of all of the schools you could have gone to, you went to your school.

Out of all of the teachers you had, you experienced the teachings of your teachers (good and bad) and had your particular style of education.

Out of all of the first jobs possible in this world, you had your job.

And, out of all of the books you could be reading right now, in this precise moment in time, **this is the book you are reading.**

So, why were you born you, in your city, in your family, in your life?

This may seem like a strange question, but it's probably the most important question you could ever ask yourself.

Why are you, you, and not anybody else?

If you can't answer the question, take some time to ponder it now for a moment.

You are the unique result of a combination of experiences, encounters, thoughts, conversations and of genes.

No one else is you.

You have experienced things in your life-time that nobody else has. What matters to you is naturally very different to what matters to the next person. So, therefore no one else knows what makes your soul feel alive but you.

So why do so many of us live lives that don't inspire us?

The last thing any of us want to do in life is live with regrets.

At times in life, we unconsciously spend our life on things we don't love. Things that often drain our energy rather than enhance our energy and this can come from a sense of duty, or obligation, or perhaps from what you experienced growing up.

That can create a situation where you feel like your life isn't going the way that you want it to. And you can even end up resenting people around you because of these unconscious choices.

Partners, bosses, friends. We 'blame others' for our situation. **But there really is only one person that can take responsibility for your life, and that person is you.** If you are in a job you don't like, it's up to you to change it.

On the other hand, each of us has things in this world that make our souls sing.

Things that energise us, that give us endless enthusiasm and energy.

Things we could do all day and not even feel hungry or tired! When I teach a course or training, I feel like I am floating on a cloud! I feel like I am doing what I was born to do.

There are unique things in this world that make your soul feel alive. Things that make your soul sing.

Remember, you could have been born ANYONE, in any life and any body.

So, be grateful for your life and your unique gifts every single day!

Truly **be grateful that you are in your life**. Whilst you may have your obstacles, you also have a LOT of opportunities and gifts that you may be overlooking.

That being said, I understand we all have challenges, but consider that these challenges have been artfully designed for you in this life based on the unique experiences that you have had.

Isn't that entirely possible?

Once I started exploring my spiritual side, I began to realise the perfection of all of the experiences (good and bad) I had had in my life, and I appreciated the opportunities of simply being born me.

CHAPTER 2: LET YOUR SOUL SING

ACTIONS

If you were to write out the top 5 unique gifts/opportunities you have experienced or received in your life, what would they be?

1. _____

2. _____

3. _____

4. _____

5. _____

Without over-thinking, write down your answer to the following question:

My spiritual beliefs are:

_____

_____

_____

KEY TAKE-AWAYS

You are unique

The clues from the above sections will help you to identify what makes your soul feel alive, and where you can mine gold from your life.

Gain a new perspective

By exploring your spiritual beliefs and appreciating the gifts and opportunities you have had from being born you, you can start to view your life through a different lens.

CHAPTER 3

It's Never Too Late

'*The greatest gift you can ever give another person is your own happiness*' – Esther Hicks

After my spiritual awakening, I started studying things that I was curious about. Neuro Linguistic Programming (NLP), meditation, healing modalities, breath work, herbal medicine, aromatherapy and yoga.

It was all very exciting and new, I just listened to the curious feeling inside of me and followed that feeling like a quest!

But underneath all the study and excitement there was still a huge problem and something I couldn't understand.

The anxiety was still there.

It started becoming more annoying and debilitating. I saw it as a hindrance that was slowing down my spiritual progress.

I kept telling myself that I needed to meditate more and that would fix things. The more I meditated, the more I became aware how dissatisfied I was with my career and my home life.

A friend who had occasional anxiety told me about essential oils that you could buy from a local health shop that helped her feel relaxed. So, I drove to the health shop one day after work, walked up to the counter and said 'I need some essential oils now!' I felt like a drug addict!

The kind woman at the counter didn't judge me at all. She suggested Lavender oil as a powerful remedy for anxiety. She told me it cost $48.

Initially I baulked at the price, but I was desperate. I handed her a $50 note, grabbed the oil and walked out to the parking lot with the tiny bottle of essential oil.

I slid into the driver's seat of my car, pulled the door shut with a thud and immediately unscrewed the cap and inhaled the scent.

Whoa.

As soon as the energy of the oil hit my nose I exploded into a waterfall of tears. I cried for at least 5, maybe 10 minutes.

Sobbing away in my expensive car with leather seats, sat-nav and automatic wipers, masking my low self-esteem.

Sobbing into my hands covered in expensive jewellery, masking my dysfunctional marriage.

Sobbing into my charcoal pantsuit which was too tight and always left unflattering button marks on my stomach at the end of a long day in the office.

Sobbing from my heart, which was opening for the first time in my life.

Sobbing from my soul.

Sobbing from my spirit.

That day — I released it all.

Finally.

Once it felt like I had cried more than I had ever cried in my life, I caught a glimpse of my own reflection in the rear view mirror. My eyes were bright green, I'd never seen them look that way before.

They sparkled.

I could finally breathe. The anxiety had subsided.

My soul, which was so close to leaving my body was alive and healed and I felt an indescribable amount of relief. I knew the anxiety was gone.

I smiled at myself, knowing that I just needed to listen to my soul from now on.

I said to myself (sounding crazy again but going along with it anyway) 'I am here now. I am listening. Tell me what to do next.'

I didn't hear anything back, but I *felt* something within me say TRUST.

****

Do you trust where you are right now in your life?

One of my clients Karina, is 57 years old and is deeply intuitive, yet she has blocked her spiritual side for her whole life, preferring to focus on raising her children.

Now, at age 57 she is curious about questions that remain unanswered.

She said to me recently 'I am just starting out on my journey now Juliet. I've raised my children. I know I've got an interesting journey ahead of me. I'm curious, but I'm not in any rush at all and I don't feel like I've left it too late'.

These days, the younger generation are delving deep into all things spiritual and metaphysical.

This is causing many people in their twenties and thirties to question the mysteries of life, the system they have been born into and whether they even need (or want) to procreate given how populated this world is already.

In my time over the past few years living and hosting retreats in Bali (which is predominantly Hindu), I have found it interesting to learn that in Hindu tradition there are four distinct stages of life experience and exploration. These stages provide a degree of focus and acceptance, which I believe is lacking in our western culture.

The first of these four stages is the schooling stage, where one acquires knowledge and builds character.

The second is the marriage stage where one enjoys good and noble things in life and raises a family.

The third stage is the ascetic or hermit stage after children are raised when they study and spend time in contemplation and meditation.

The Ashrama is the final stage in life in which one renounces all worldly ties and ponders the mysteries of life. This is an age of wisdom and in this age they are taken care of by their families.

Ponder what your life would have been like if you simply knew and trusted this path for yourself, and the times in your life to explore different areas, as many Hindu's do.

They know, in their thirties for example, there is little need to question the mysteries of life, because they are busy raising a family and there is time to ponder that later.

If you compare this to our Western society it is a very different reality. There is no clear path anymore.

This is a double-edged sword.

With no clear path for how we should live our lives, there is confusion about next about everything.

Diets, career paths, relationships, finances. There is an overload of pressure, information and comparison in the world today. Less of us are starting families and going to university, and more of us are seeking higher levels of fulfilment, evolution and enlightenment.

However, with all these choices we also have the beauty of the freedom to question our societal programming and create a new life for ourselves with a new paradigm.

This shift is evolution.

Each of us needs to focus and say no to what no longer serves us (or the world) and find the path that feels right within.

When we as individuals find and follow that path the entire world benefits.

When we listen to our heart *as well as* our head.

It takes courage to do this and to step outside what is comfortable and known.

There is no manual to life aside from the guidance that lives within your eternal being.

So, whatever seeds have been planted in your life and are now starting to sprout, and whatever has led you to holding this book in your hand, allow it and trust that it is never too late for the dream that lives inside of you.

What if the dream that lives inside of you is the very thing that many others in this world are looking for?

Imagine that the dream you have inside you is part of another soul's quest.

Like a jigsaw puzzle. Everything in this world is interconnected.

What if until you bring your dream out into the world, that gift that lies dormant within you, another person's gift cannot be born?

For example, today I spent the morning with one of my beautiful clients Carol.

Carol quit her Government job of over a decade last month, recently moved house and is in the process of finding what makes her soul sing.

Recently we sat down to write her new resume and cover letter for a job in order to begin a career in the wellness industry.

At the end of our session she was teary and she said I could have never done this without you!

The following week she found a job in a holistic wellness clinic and called me excitedly to tell me the good news! My heart burst with happiness that I was able to help her put that jigsaw piece together.

I share this with you because I do often wonder; what if I had just taken the 'safe' option in my life and not pursued this life and business I have today?

Who would be supporting Carol and all my other clients on their journeys to pursue their dreams right now?

How would the world be different?

Each class I teach I see people physically and emotionally release tension and worry from their bodies.

Each client session I run I see enhanced clarity and vision and strength. I see light-bulb moments and connection to higher selves.

And each course I run I see people gaining perspective, meeting their soul families and achieving life-changing transformations.

I know I am making a difference, and that's what keeps me going when I am challenged in my business and in my life.

So I ask you — what if that dream that lives inside you could be helping someone in the world, just as I helped Carol?

If your dreams fit into the world like a jigsaw puzzle, I wonder who is waiting for your piece to be placed on the board before they can see where their piece fits?

And if you feel as if you've left it too late, or you're too far into your career already, remember it's never too late to start the journey of redesigning your life.

Louise L. Hay started Hay House Publishing in 1984 at the age of 58. An incredibly inspiring woman who did not let her abusive childhood and traumatic experiences growing up to deter her from her life's purpose. She has changed the life of millions around the world and continues to do so. (Hay House Publishing: http://www.hayhouse.com.au/)

Her life's work had only really begun 15 years prior.

She had to endure a painful lifetime of lessons including healing her own cancer before she could transform her message into the life-changing platform she has brought to the world today. It was through these challenges and obstacles that she has been able to dedicate herself to her teachings, and bring immense healing to a troubled world.

As a result she started the publishing house that has given a voice to incredible teachers such as Dr Wayne Dyer, Dr Christiane Northrup and Doreen Virtue.

We aren't all about to start publishing companies, but what this tells me is that it's never too late for any of us to start pursuing what makes our soul sing.

It is important to know that we all have seeds planted throughout our lives, and sometimes the harvests are collected later in life. Sometimes, though, you simply know that it's time to start trusting the signs and get the courage to say yes to your dreams.

KEY TAKE-AWAYS

- Trust that everything is happening as it should be.
- If your message seems strange or different, it's because the world is asking for it. It means there are people seeking what you have to offer.
- Your dreams are a piece of the jigsaw puzzle of this perfect world. Stop holding yourself back by living in fear and procrastination.

ACTION

Without over-thinking write down your answer to the following question:

How would you truly love to make a difference in this world?

CHAPTER 4

_____

_____

You Deserve to Live Your Happiest and Most Fulfilling Life

'In your moments of decision, your destiny is shaped.'
– Tony Robbins

On the 21st of September 2013 I made the difficult decision to leave my marriage. I walked away from the man who had been by my side since I was 16 years old.

The moment had been building subconsciously for a while, but I finally had realised I could not live one more day in the passionless life we had co-created.

Beforehand I wrote out a letter to get my thoughts straight.

Fear and judgement ran through my head, threatening to halt me back into security.

I thought to myself 'But I've been with him since I was 16... he has always kept me safe. We are married, I can't get divorced, what about all the people who came to my wedding? How embarrassing. What will they think?'

'What about all my single girlfriends who tell me there are no good men out there? Are they right? Does this mean I'll be alone forever and perhaps even never have kids?'

I had to accept all of my worst fears.

I accepted the fact that I may never have children.

I accepted the fact that I may be alone forever.

I accepted the fact that I may receive judgement from people in my life.

As I imagined the rest of my life, I saw two paths laid out in front of me.

The first was set in stone.

I imagined my future if I stayed with my husband.

We would have two kids, and in 10 years time I would probably still be in the same job, and be bitter, miserable and overweight. My heart sank and I felt heavy when I imagined our life in the future.

The second path was completely unwritten.

It was a blank canvas.

My heart skipped at the excitement and curiosity of this undiscovered life.

I knew I wanted to paint that canvas myself.

I admit — I was petrified!

But the decision had been made.

I knew what to do.

I wanted to redesign my future. I wanted a second chance at life.

The day I drove out of our driveway with a few things packed in my car I felt free. For the first time in my adult life I was on my own and in charge of my own life.

I stayed in an apartment by the beach, a short-term holiday apartment. I journaled at the beach for most of the afternoon and each word I wrote confirmed that I had made the right decision.

I asked myself 'have I learned all that I need to from this relationship?', 'are we better off as friends?' and 'am I willing to accept that he may move on and find someone else?' and all my answers pointed to a firm and calm yes.

After journaling for a few hours I stood up to walk to the local supermarket to buy some supplies for dinner and I realised, smiling to myself 'I can buy exactly what I feel like for dinner and there is no one else to think of but myself!' what a thrill.

On the way home, a tall, handsome man on a motorbike pulled over the side of the road and as he removed his helmet our eyes locked. I smiled, openly and energetically to him and felt a rush of energy through my entire body as he smiled back at me.

It was the first time I had flirted with a man in over ten years. It felt incredible, and very scary at the same time! "Slow down Juliet, I told myself!" I quickly closed my energy down and scurried off home.

By evening, a rollercoaster of emotions had washed over me.

I questioned if I had made a big mistake leaving... but I never felt like going back.

I just felt afraid and suddenly, very alone for the first time in my entire life.

I sank into my fears and felt them all.

Raw and real, finally being authentic with myself.

I looked up at the sky and asked if I had made the right decision.

As the universe always does, when we ask for guidance, I was sent a clear signal.

I looked across to the tissue box to blow my nose and wipe away my silent tears and noticed there was just one book sitting on the nightstand.

The Alchemist by Paulo Coehlo stared back at me. I had been meaning to read it for years.

I smiled knowingly, reached over and opened it, and pulled out the well-worn bookmark that was carefully placed in the front cover.

I read it, from start to finish that night.

Around midnight I was halfway through and I read the words 'maktub.'

I smiled and looked up at the ceiling.

I said aloud **'maktub.'**

"It is written."

All of life, it is written.

I immediately felt at ease about my decision.

A few months later I went to Bali and took myself on a 7 day yoga retreat in the spiritual centre of Bali, Ubud.

During the retreat we were guided through a process of 24 hours of silence. During the silent day I wrote:

JOURNAL ENTRY

I am sitting at my desk in Ubud on silent day of the yoga retreat.

I feel so free. I have just written out my bucket list and I feel excited about my future!

I want to buy an apartment by the beach.
I want to travel through Europe and America.
I want to start my own business in a few years – doing what I have NO idea!

I just trust that everything is going to be okay.
I have no idea what I'm doing actually but all I know is now I am doing things that FEEL good to me.

By the time the sun set over the rice fields in Ubud I had written so much that I used up three pens and had black ink running down my fingers.

I thought to myself *Wow, wouldn't it be amazing to run retreats in Bali one day, just like this for women who are at turning points in their lives! And perhaps one day I could even write a book!*

Immediately I crushed my dreams myself, saying to myself 'Who would want to go on a retreat with you?' and 'your story isn't interesting enough to write a book about…!' Imagine if I had listened to that inner dream crusher…

****

Leaving my marriage was a difficult decision, one that caused a ripple effect on my life and on my husband's life. Difficult decisions are a fact of life.

But not deciding is also a decision.

If I had stayed, I would have made a decision by default.

I would have created a family based on fear of the unknown and ignoring my feelings and those conditions would have cascaded down to my children.

And it would have been so unfair to them, and to my husband. As I write this book he is now remarried and I am truly happy for him.

Sometimes the indecision is the hardest part.

Once we make a decision we can take action, move forward and start making change.

The feeling of being in limbo is a horrible feeling.

We 'to and fro' and end up living in a perpetual state of fear of the unknown.

I am lucky that I left my husband on the day I made the conscious decision. The decision had been building unconsciously for months, perhaps even years, but on the day I decided - I left.

I didn't sit on the decision for weeks, months or years, thus dragging out the pain for both of us.

I am not telling you to end your current relationship. I am telling you to commit fully to whatever decision you have made!

Either fully commit to your relationship or be fully free of your relationship. Either be fully in your job or fully planning your way out of it. No more indecision and complaining and staying stuck. No more living out decisions with one foot in one foot out.

Because a sure way to ruin a relationship (or a job) is to have a part of you wishing you weren't there.

What I do know is that our relationships, jobs and all of life reflect ourselves back to us.

You can only feel loved in your relationship to the level that you love yourself.

You can only feel fulfilled in your job to the level that you feel fulfilled personally.

And you can only feel supported and valued by someone to the degree that you are supporting and valuing yourself.

So, what stops us from making difficult decisions in order to live our happiest lives?

I've already spoken about living for others, from fear or from a sense of obligation.

Later in the book in the chapter titled 'Fear is an Illusion' I will break down the fears that sometimes do hold us back. Those fears can actually be useful (if used properly).

But in this chapter I am going to focus on procrastination and indecision.

Procrastinating over a decision is a way of creating a significant amount of unconscious stress in your mind.

And the more your headspace is full of stress and doubt and worry the less you are able to focus on the future and your dreams.

If you are carrying around stress then your body is full of cortisol and your mind is unable to make effective decisions. In my studies with *Heartmath*TM, I learned about the power of meditation and heart-focused breathing to reduce stress and enable us to think more clearly.

This happens as a result of being in flow, and enhancing Dehydroepiandrosterone (DHEA) which is a hormone that comes from the adrenal gland and reduces cortisol. When we have cortisol in our system our defence mechanisms are heightened and we perceive literally everything as a threat. And then any chance you have of making a decision based on what your 'heart' wants is significantly impacted.

What decisions are currently sitting in your 'inbox' waiting to be handled?

What are you procrastinating on or about? *And why?*

Take a deep breath, and be honest with yourself.

How would it feel to make a decision and simply move forward?

One way or the other.

Did you know that there is such a thing as 'decision fatigue?'

It's a term for exceeding the maximum amount of quality decisions you can make in a given day.

On average, research has shown that we make over 200 decisions each day just on food choices alone! What a waste of our decision making horse-power.

And even more surprisingly, statistics have shown that if you add up all the time women spend on average deciding what to wear, it would equate to 287 days - that's almost an entire year!

So it's no wonder when it comes to something as critical as figuring out our life purpose, we are too tired at the end of the day, or can't make a quality level of decision!

Not to mention, so many of us are energy depleted through poor sleep, nutrition and a lack of focus (which we will delve into in the next chapter when I share my 'Five Keys To Fulfilment' with you).

When you combine poor sleep, with decision fatigue and excess cortisol in our blood-stream and pressure from work, relationships, finances, etc. it's no wonder so many of us are struggling to live the life of our dreams!

So, decide now to take action on your dreams so you can start living your dream life.

So you can start saying 'yes' to your dreams and to showing up, to look after yourself and your future and to start making high quality decisions.

Remember, the decisions you make today shape your tomorrow.

The day I left my marriage I sent a clear message that my life was fully in my hands. It was a powerful moment for me.

Since then, I have made many, many brave decisions in business and life. Such as firing a retreat venue that wasn't at the standard I required, hiring an expensive office space, and deciding to run life-changing events and overseas retreats for women to pursue their dreams.

When it comes to all decisions in life, we can only ever make two choices:

- The first choice – is to change the situation
- If you can't change it, the second choice is to accept the situation as it is.

Whatever you do, commit to one or the other – stop living in limbo!

Change or accept.

That's all there is.

Start living in the driver's seat of your life.

KEY TAKE-AWAYS:

- Be fully committed to all areas of your life
- Our relationships with others reflect the relationship we have with ourselves
- In our moments of decision, our destiny is shaped
- Change or accept everything in your life.

ACTION:

What are you procrastinating about at the moment?

_____

_____

_____

What is one action or decision you are avoiding making, and what can you decide to do today?

CHAPTER 5

_____

_____

_____

The 5 Keys to Fulfilment

'What lies behind us and what lies before us are tiny matters compared to what lies within us.' – Ralph Waldo Emerson

In September 2013, a few weeks after I left my marriage I moved into a big, expensive apartment by the beach. I enjoyed filling it with beautiful, modern furniture chosen only by me.

It was an old school building by the beach which had been renovated into modern loft-style apartments, with a big original blackboard in the open plan kitchen.

It was light-filled, had high ceilings and a huge grand entertaining kitchen.

It was a magical place to assert my single status to the world.

It was fun making all the decisions on my own house and it was equally important for me to show the world I was 'safe and successful' on my own.

But I wasn't on my own for long. A few weeks after I left my husband, despite all logic and reason I fell into the arms of an older man.

We shared a beautiful romance that lasted for nearly six months and I relied on him for support through those initial months of navigating the world for the first time without my husband. It would have been easy to stay with him. He offered me security, wisdom, freedom and devotion. And although we loved one another, somewhere deep within my soul I knew we wouldn't be together forever.

I still had so much of the world to explore and learn about, *I felt like my life was only just beginning.*

Some people come into our lives to teach us for a short time, others a long time. And we definitely healed one another's hearts during our romance.

It was a beautiful time of opening, of learning about the world and I remember saying to myself often *'thank you Juliet!'* For the choice I had made to begin the process of redesigning my life.

****

In those first few months I felt the first few glimpses of my own fulfilment in rebuilding my life.

Initially I thought it was the apartment and a passionate love life that made me feel fulfilled! In hindsight I realise what was truly fulfilling was that I was finally making my own decisions.

There is no doubt that the freedom to make my own decisions gave (and still gives me) a deep sense of fulfilment.

But that may not be the same for us all.

In this chapter I am going to introduce you to a concept I call, the ''Five Keys to Fulfilment' which will help you uncover how to live your most fulfilling life. These keys will provide you with perspective and guidelines for you to follow in rebuilding your life, They will also simplify the things you need to unlock in order to feel fulfilled.

Before I explain the keys I want to remind you that fulfilment means different things to us all.

Some people are deeply fulfilled by having children, whilst others are fulfilled by earning a six-figure income.

And some people feel fulfilled by these things up to a certain point.

A change. An awakening. Some may call it a spiritual awakening, or a mid-life crisis.

Being fulfilled is also about knowing that you are happy and contented from within.

And it truly is different for everyone.

For me, fulfilment is a state of inner peace and a sense of knowing that you have developed (and continue to develop) into what is your highest potential in life. Moving into the apartment and leaving my marriage were the first steps towards me living a life of my highest potential.

A continual development towards our highest potential represents the successful result of gently following our own unique dreams in a way which also supports us to live a life in accordance to our values.

Because what makes your soul feel alive and fulfilled is so different to what makes anyone else feel alive and fulfilled.

And what constitutes a 'life well lived' on your terms is different for us all — because what is important to you in life is unique only to you.

Ultimately however, fulfilment is a state. An emotion. A feeling.

And with all feelings, it's possible to feel it now. Let me show you what I mean by this simple activity that you can do now.

ACTIVITY

Close your eyes, take a deep breath and imagine for a moment how it would feel to be deeply fulfilled.

How does your body feel when you imagine feeling fulfilled?

(e.g. what sensations or responses do you have in your physical body?)

You may have felt relaxed after this exercise, or even open and receptive. If you had difficulty with this exercise, take a deep breath and try again.

Remember, fulfilment is something that starts as a feeling inside of you.

It is not something to seek outside of you.

It's possible to feel fulfilled all the time by following the simple exercise you just completed. It will take time, but if done regularly you will work your way towards a life where this feeling is a daily reality.

My vision for you through reading this book is to have peace in where you are right now, to be making a difference in the way that feels best to you; and to enjoy your most fulfilling life through developing your highest potential.

Whatever this means for you.

As mentioned, through my pursuit of my own desire to become fulfilled, I have built a model and framework which I call the 'Five Keys to Fulfilment.'

These five keys are powerful because they can assist you to stop, take a moment to review your life, and assess where you are presently.

By assessing where you are right now, you can also see how you can maintain and develop your highest potential moving forward.

By maintaining and developing your highest potential, you continually gain access to connect to the state of fulfilment within you.

Each key comes with a set of activities you can follow, to review which ones you may want to work further on in order to unlock your most fulfilling life.

These keys will help you uncover areas where you may need to make some decisions that will improve the quality of your life, or help you become unstuck.

I encourage you to review these as often as possible and if you'd like to explore these further I invite you to join my Relaunch My Life online course, at www.julietlever.com which walks you through each one.

The Five Keys To Fulfilment are:

- Vitality
  (self care and self talk)

- Victories
  (self esteem and self belief)

- Variety
  (self expansion and experiences)

- Value
  (self alignment and self worth)

- Vision
  (self direction)

KEY NUMBER 1

Vitality
(Self care)

If you feel low, lethargic and negative, how much do you care about feeling fulfilled? Not much. You feel uninspired and low of energy.

And how does it feel when you feel like this first thing in the morning?

Not much of a foundation to build a fulfilling day or future on is it?

On the other hand, how does it feel to have a quality of life and energy, organised and inspired life force that enables you to focus on things that bring you joy?

Where you have all the energy to jump out of bed and feel inspired and excited about the life you have created?

When you have a strong mental vitality that enables you to make conscious decisions and pursue your dreams?

Trust me — it feels incredible!

It wasn't until my late twenties that I started to take care of my physical body.

Now, my energy and vitality is number one! And yoga is a daily practice and is the foundation of my vitality. To me, yoga is separate to a work out. It's more of a body and breath connection than a physical exercise connection. I train weights at the gym 2-3 times per week, walk every day and practice yoga daily.

I encourage all of my clients to ensure they have a daily routine that supports them to feel alive.

You can't give from an empty cup.

We all know this, but it still surprises me how few people have mastered the art of self-care as a priority.

Starting the day with a walk in nature, a big glass of lemon water, or a yoga and meditation practice is so simple, yet profoundly life-changing.

If you are serious about living your most fulfilling life then self-care as a constant in your life is a non-negotiable.

Vitality does not only apply to our physical body, but also within the vitality in our thoughts and emotions.

ACTIVITY

How would you rate your level of self-care and self-talk at present?

_____

_____

_____

What changes to your daily rituals or habits do you need to make starting NOW to support your highest vitality?

_____

_____

_____

So, the first key to fulfilment is self care, or VITALITY. It is from this foundation that we can build upwards to the second key.

KEY NUMBER 2

Victories
(Self esteem and self belief)

Once we feel balanced physically, we also need to be feeling fulfilled mentally and emotionally.

If you experience low self-esteem you can easily fall into a downward spiral and also form a habit of constantly seeking external praise.

If you feel like you aren't enough, you can tire yourself out trying to please others or worry about what others will say or think about you. Low self-esteem leads to a waste of energy and time on things that you cannot control.

On the other hand, if you have a healthy level of self-esteem and feel safe and confident within yourself then you feel inspired to take risks and make choices based on what feels right for you. Based on what you believe is possible.

Developing and building a healthy level of self-esteem and belief is possible by focusing on your successes in life rather than always focusing on failures.

Yet so often, we remember our failures and forget all about our successes.

Focusing on your successes and self praise is essential to a fulfilling life. So let's take some time to build your self-esteem in this moment.

ACTIVITY:

What is one of the proudest moments from your life? Why?

_____

_____

_____

What is one of the most powerful actions you have ever taken? Why?

_____

_____

_____

Notice what your answers to the above two questions tell you about yourself. Perhaps you are more aware of a side of yourself that you may not have valued until now.

Learn to regularly praise yourself.

Start being your own cheerleader, because you are going to be your own best friend for a long time!

Praise yourself, because life is hard enough without being your own worst critic.

The second key to fulfilment is self esteem and belief, and I encourage you to praise yourself and celebrate your wins as often as you can.

KEY NUMBER 3

Variety
(Self experiences and expansion)

Have you ever seen the eighties movie 'Groundhog Day?' In the movie, Bill Murray gets stuck in the same day over and over again. The beautiful message in this movie is that so many people do live the same existence over and over with few new experiences. How boring would that be?

According to motivational expert Tony Robbins, one of our six human needs is the need for a balance between variety and certainty.

If we have too much variety or uncertainty, we become unstable and feel unsafe. If we have too much certainty we seek adventure.

So providing yourself with an array of new experiences will teach and challenge you in a variety of new ways.

How you approach and handle new experiences will also teach you about yourself and give you a beautiful platform to be able to take on new challenges. This also means being able to explore different solutions to challenges in life.

Challenges are a part of life and the ability to handle them in a variety of ways is a key to fulfilment.

When we try new things we develop new neural pathways and open up to new possibilities.

In the few months after leaving my marriage, I said YES to as many things as I possibly could. I went to evening self development classes, I went belly dancing, when my next-door neighbour told me she was going Dragon Boat Racing and asked if I'd like to come, I said 'Yes' even though I didn't know what it was! I put myself in as many different situations as I could and I grew outside my usual comfort zone and learned a lot in the process.

This key also extends to expanding our thoughts and encouraging ourselves to think in a variety of ways.

So, let's look at how much variety you have in your life right now.

ACTIVITY:

What is something that slightly scares you that you want to try?

_____

_____

What is something new you have done in the past 6 months?

_____

_____

Do you find it easy to think of a variety of different solutions to one problem?

_____

Let's test that out. Imagine you had to come up with $5000 within 2 days.

What are 3 ways you could do this (*legally of course!*)?

_____

_____

_____

Key 3 is about variety, not only in relation to experiences but to how many ways we can expand our thinking to solve the challenges and problems we face in life.

This key is a truly liberating one! Remember, you only get one life, and you are in the driver's seat.

Life experience teaches us so much more than words ever can. So step outside your comfort zone and start adding more variety to your life!

KEY NUMBER 4

Values

(Self alignment and self worth)

How aware are you of your own inner alignment?

And what is self-awareness anyway? To me, self-awareness is having conscious knowledge and awareness of your own thoughts, personality and emotions. And how you choose to interact with the world.

It is a challenging skill to master. I wonder if it's possible to master self awareness at all, or if it's more of a practice, such as the Art of Zen.

How often do you objectively assess your decisions and actions without casting blame on yourself or others?

When I started my journey of self-discovery I studied many different perspectives on growing myself and my self-awareness.

If you look at things from a Zen philosophy, we are nothing more than the conscious awareness operating in our own body. You are the awareness looking through your own eyes.

From a place of self awareness, you can make decisions based on things that are important to you and start to understand and appreciate your values.

The reason this key is so important to fulfilment is that if your life is not in alignment with your values then there is a high chance that you are going to feel unfulfilled.

Too often, the people we clash most with in life are the very people who have conflicting values to our own.

For example, a boss may have a high value on career and money and not see eye-to-eye with an employee who they are trying to get to stay back for work. Despite being offered to be paid double time, the employee, who has a higher value on spending time with their family may choose to decline. Neither party is right or wrong, it's just a difference of values. Yet, both parties probably feel frustrated at the other.

Our values do shift over time and this is normal, so I encourage you to come back to the Five Keys to Fulfilment regularly to ensure you are on your path and living in alignment with your values.

ACTIVITY:

Find your values

What is important to you in life?

List as many as you can, and then circle your top 3

_____

_____

_____

_____

Which of your values are currently being compromised or questioned (if any)? Where are you out of alignment?

_____

_____

_____

Find your worth

The hidden key to value also extends to _valuing yourself, your time and your energy._

Time really is your most precious resource, because you can never get it back again. Money can be earned again, but time, once spent, is gone forever.

Other people in your life will only value you (and your time) to the extent that you value yourself e.g. when you get an hour of alone time do you:

- Answer work emails and check social media?
- Watch television?
- Go for a walk in nature or take a bath?

Notice which one you would have picked and notice what that says about your values and how much you value your time and energy?

Whether or not you are planning to change careers it is important for you to calculate how much your time is worth in dollar terms. So many of us believe that our worth is what our workplace is currently paying us! I promise you, it's much higher than that.

Knowing your worth helps with making intelligent and self confident decisions in all areas of life.

This exercise has helped many of my clients determine their hourly rate for their new businesses, say no to clients who undervalue their time or negotiate raises confidently at work.

How do you find your worth in dollar terms?

First Step: Select something you love to do every day that takes roughly an hour. *It could be a walk at the beach, practicing yoga, or sharing a meal with a loved one.*

_____

Second Step: How much would someone have to pay you to take away that activity from your day? How much would it take for you to do what they wanted over what you truly love to do?

$_____per hour

This should give you an indication of your worth in dollar terms.

If I am ever working on something or with a client and think 'I would rather be at the beach right now' then I know I haven't valued myself enough or it's not the right use of my time and energy.

Another area to examine is your friendships. Sometimes we hold onto friendships that no longer serve our time and energy. You are allowed to spend your time in ways that energise you. Never spend time with someone because of guilt. So before agreeing to see someone who drains your energy it is important to ask yourself 'Would I rather have an hour to myself, or spend an hour with this person?' If the answer is that you would rather have an hour to yourself, then you know what to do.

ACTIVITY:

How can you value your time and energy more? Starting today.

_____

_____

_____

KEY NUMBER 5

Vision
(Self Direction)

This last key is crucial. It's the final piece of the puzzle.

It is vital that you have a clear vision stated in positive terms for your future, your well-being and your self-direction in life.

If you don't know where you're heading or what you believe is possible for you, then you can bob around aimlessly, floating around and feeling lost at sea, moving from opportunity to opportunity, relationship to relationship, dabbling your way through life and never really making anything work.

This can lead you to a life where you feel you have missed the boat!

However, if you decide today to start having a clear vision then you can know where your ship is headed, you can set the course and allow the wind and conditions to take you there.

The way our mind works, it is split into two parts — our conscious mind and our unconscious mind.

Our conscious mind is responsible for about 5% of

our behaviours and actions, whereas our unconscious mind is 95% of our thoughts, beliefs, feelings, emotions and actions.

For example, have you ever consciously decided to start a diet, only to catch yourself day-dreaming about all the delicious food you are craving all day? That's the difference between our conscious and unconscious minds. Our unconscious mind will always surface and bring to the forefront what we want deep down.

Now, if you did some work on your unconscious mind to associate unhealthy food to diabetes, self sabotage or obesity you may find that those day-dreams change. That's the type of work I do with my clients and students.

Matching their conscious dreams and goals to their unconscious mind, so that 100% of their body mind and spirit is travelling in the same direction towards desired outcomes; rather than a lifetime of self sabotage and unfulfilled dreams.

So that being said, if you imagine that your conscious mind is the ship that sets the vision, then your unconscious mind is everything that will support the ship to obtain the vision (the boat, the crew, the conditions, the wind direction).

Visualisation is an extremely powerful way of using

your unconscious mind and imagination for a creative and constructive purpose.

The reason we want a purpose to work towards is it gives our busy and hungry mind high quality thoughts to chew on. If you have no vision then your mind is going to dig about in the corners of your dusty psyche for any old thoughts that it can chew on for as long as possible.

A positive and exciting vision is a recipe for a healthy and long lasting life.

Now, in order to maintain your motivation for your vision you must ensure that your vision for anything in life **is in alignment with your values and beliefs.**

Many times I have worked with clients who have a vision for their future, but it's not actually based on a future they want deep down, but instead a future that someone else wants for them. Or a future they think they 'should' have rather than one that they want.

Your subconscious mind will always protect you from moving towards a situation you unconsciously don't want.

One of my clients who first came to me with very low self-esteem Alana told me about a time in her life when she felt like she 'failed' because she didn't do well at university studying law.

When I explored with her more, she admitted that she hated the dry legal subjects and was only studying law because her parents wanted her to and everyone else in her family was a lawyer. She realised in our session that she failed the exam because unconsciously she wanted to! If she had passed her exams she would now be a lawyer, perhaps overworked and unhappy!

Her values in life are nature, self development and art — not law and career! No wonder she self-sabotaged! Alana was able to see that past viewed 'failure' as a true success and gift for her in her life. And she was grateful to herself for failing the exam!

Have you got a vision or goal that you are working towards that you have struggled to take action on? Is it possible that there are some subconscious beliefs that could be holding back that vision?

ACTIVITY:

Think about a perceived failure from your past and how it has actually helped you in your life today.

_____

_____

_____

Write out a vision for your life where you will be in 3 years time, make it as imaginative as possible and visualise it for 5 minutes, with a smile on your face!

_____

_____

_____

_____

_____

What underlying fears or doubts arise when you think of this vision?

_____

_____

_____

SUMMARY

The Five Keys to Fulfilment have unlocked my happiness and the happiness of my clients. They are a powerful way of aligning yourself to what you truly want in life and working on any areas that are holding you back.

Using these keys enables you to tailor a map to fulfilment for your own life. When you have a map you have a guide to show you the way that is in alignment with your soul's purpose.

At my live events and retreats we workshop these Five Keys to assist you to explore where you are fulfilled in each area and where you may in fact have some blind spots.

The Five Keys to Fulfilment are the secret to unlocking your most fulfilled life and they will help you to make the right decisions for you.

****

Now, if you skipped over the five key to fulfilment questions, take some time to step back and fill them out now.

They will give you a window to your soul and answering them will bring you one step closer to your most fulfilled life.

ACTION TAKE AWAY

Complete all of the questions in the five keys to fulfilment and review these regularly.

Bonus: Visit www.julietlever.com.au to find out more about my courses and trainings which allow you to understand more about creating alignment.

CHAPTER 6

Reconnect To Your Soul

"The two hardest tests on the spiritual road are the patience to wait for the right moment and the courage not to be disappointed with what we encounter." – Paulo Coelho

In those first few months in late 2013 after leaving my marriage I went on a rollercoaster ride of freedom, fulfilment and fun. My ex-husband and I separated our assets amicably and he and I both moved on.

But, in the quiet of my solitude I felt unsure about my future.

Logically, I reassured myself by saying 'At least I am earning lots of money and have a stable job I have been at for nearly 7 years! I am safe. I just got a pay-rise and bonus the previous month. Nothing to worry about!'

And then, just like that - **the universe sent me a curveball.**

With a startling crash back to reality, things changed in an instant at work. Even though I had just received a significant pay increase and bonus in my recent annual review, my boss had decided that I needed to be replaced with a more experienced manager.

I was essentially demoted.

It seemed the universe wanted me to follow my soul's purpose sooner than I was ready to.

Sometimes when we don't follow our path, or we try to stay in a comfort zone we get pushed - with a great big shove!

Apparently, although I had been a pivotal part in growing the department I managed from 5 staff to 50 over 6 years, I needed to be replaced with someone with *more experience* based on where the company was heading in the future.

My ego took a big hit.

I handled it as gracefully as I could. But beneath the strong facade I was petrified and felt cast aside by the company I had helped grow from a small company with 30 staff to a national brand with over 300. It was a humbling experience to go through.

I had a huge apartment and car loan to pay for. I didn't have a second income to rely on anymore. Suddenly, I felt very vulnerable and very, very alone. The pressure was on and I stepped back into my masculine side to cope. I started to over-eat and over-exercise again to compensate with the fear I felt inside. My anxiety came back with a vengeance.

I trawled job seeker websites but nothing sparked any interest.

All the jobs seemed the same to me.

Targets. Measurements. Pressure. Stress. Selling yourself. Tailoring your resume to 'fit the job.'

To me I felt like I was in a prison.

I knew I wanted to make a bigger impact on the world than just making a company lots of money. And I knew that if I had been treated this way after six years of loyalty to this company, then there was very little 'security' in any company I could work in in the future. Sometimes we seek what seems to be the safe option, but it isn't safe at all.

I wanted to be free.

I knew deep down I was born to serve a greater purpose.

I was sick of the corporate life, but I had no idea how to escape it.

Working in an office was all I had ever known since I finished school and I couldn't see how any of my skills could be transferrable to anything of value.

The idea of starting my own business was absolutely terrifying. This was probably because all I had ever heard about was statistics and accounts of how many small businesses fail!

I tried not to put too much pressure on myself to rush into anything, but work started getting more and more unbearable as the weeks went by.

They had trouble recruiting my replacement, and I was still managing my sales team and responsible for their results for months with the fear of the unknown looming in the distance. It was a challenge just to go to work. I was tempted to go out on stress leave but didn't want to taint my personal brand. Everyone in my team looked up at me as an inspiring and confident leader, and I couldn't let them all down.

To get myself through the work-days I spent most of my weekly wage on massages during my lunch breaks, getting my nails done, occasional chocolate treats and expensive clothes to cheer myself up.

I guess that's the real cost of not following your purpose... you have to find temporary ways to cheer yourself up and distract yourself from the truth.

However, it's always a short-term fix.

It's never enough when your soul is unfulfilled...

****

Although it felt like my world was falling apart at the time, I was very fortunate to have lost all of my identities in a very short timeframe.

I removed my 'wife' label.

I removed my 'executive/corporate' label.

I know there was a very real chance I could have experienced a complete breakdown (and I can now completely understand why some people do!).

I hung on by a thread at times in my journey of self-discovery.

It was incredibly scary to lose everything that I thought I was. It is only now that I realise that I was able to let go of all the parts of me that weren't really even me to begin with.

In the process, I made space for the new to come into my life.

The end of my marriage and the demotion at work gave me the biggest opportunity. It gave me the opportunity to relaunch my life.

I realise now that everything was happening for me, not to me.

I firmly believe that with the benefit of hindsight, if something wasn't meant to be happening in your life, it wouldn't be happening.

It feels horrible at the time, believe me I know! But once you get past it, you can see the wisdom in the chaos.

The universe was orchestrating things for me and my 'wake up call,' my courage to leave my husband, my demotion at work, it was all to get me to a life where I am now living an authentic life and I am fully in the driver's seat.

At times, when I was close to losing it all and having a breakdown, all I would do is focus on my breath.

This would connect me to my heart and in turn to my soul.

In my most challenging moments I called upon the following process which I still use today when something stops me and causes me to contemplate and grow.

I call this process 'Reconnect To Your Soul.'

It's so simple, but it is profound.

This process allows you to connect deep within yourself, to your inner guidance system and to your sense of knowing.

Reconnect To Your Soul is a technique that has also helped numerous clients of mine when they have been experiencing severe anxiety as it helps them to learn to interpret their bodies and to understand their unique signals.

RECONNECT TO YOUR SOUL

Step 1)   Place your hands on your heart, palm down.

Step 2)   Close your eyes and breathe deeply three times.

Step 3)   Out loud, ask 'heart, what have you been trying to tell me,' or 'Soul, what do you need to say to me?'

Step 4)   Listen with your feelings.

You may receive words.

You may receive a feeling

You may receive images.

Allow whatever arises without judgement.

Practice this step daily to build your connection to yourself and to reconnect to your soul.

Allow it to come.

If you cannot hear anything, then try again and listen closer.

Be still and quiet and listen. Slow down.

Allow yourself to receive.

Souls whisper, they never shout.

For a moment, consider that this state of connection is in fact your natural state. Our natural state of being is a state of relaxation — open, connected, loving inner peace.

At one of my Bali retreats one year one of my beautiful guests said to me on the second to last day 'Oh Juliet, I'm going to try to hold on to this feeling as long as I possibly can when I get home!'

I explained to her lovingly, 'There is nothing to hold onto! This is your natural state.'

"Our natural state of being is a state of being relaxed, open, connected and of inner peace."

We often get glimpses of this when we go on holiday.

For a moment, cast your memory back to the last holiday you took *(hopefully it wasn't too long ago!)*.

How did you feel when you were on holiday?

Did you unwind?

Did you open?

Did you relax?

Take a moment to remember a specific moment from this holiday and place a smile on your face and breathe.

This is your natural state of inner peace.

Our modern lifestyle often causes us to disconnect from our natural state.

Expectations, technology, being indoors for hours on end and living for others causes us to live lives that rarely align with our soul's purpose. If we are stressed, pressured or blocked then we cannot receive the opportunities and magic that is trying to find us. When we are stressed or pressured it's like we are a lighthouse with no light on.

Make a choice to surrender and release ALL expectations of yourself. And connect to the peaceful, luminous truth that resides inside. That way the magic of what you truly want can sail safely towards your shining light.

ACTIVITY:

Practice the 'Reconnect To Your Soul' process as often as possible for 7 days.

Practice using this technique with simple exercises such as what to eat for lunch, or what form of exercise to do so you can build this strength.

Above all, you will learn far more from experience than from words on a page.

Practice this yourself, and learn from your own experience how deeply you can connect with your own soul.

Notes from practicing the process:

_____

_____

_____

KEY TAKE-AWAYS

- Consider how much it is costing you not to pursue what makes your soul feel alive.
- Take time to connect to practice 'Reconnect Your Soul' as often as you can.
- Check in regularly to sense if your energy is shining brightly in your natural relaxed, open and connected state.

CHAPTER 7

Redesign Your Future

'We must be willing to let go of the life we planned so as to have the life that is waiting for us.' – Joseph Campbell

On ANZAC Day, April 25th, 2014 my grandmother passed away. I cried for hours when I heard the news.

Her funeral was on May 1st, which also happened to be my 28th birthday.

It was a bittersweet feeling, arriving to the chapel and seeing weeping friends and family and then have them wish me a happy birthday through the sadness in their eyes.

The symbolism of the timing was not lost on me.

My grandmother signified a woman in my life who was powerful, giving and intelligent.

I was finally ready to be that woman for myself.

I was giving birth to the powerful, giving and intelligent Juliet on my birthday. A torch I would gladly take over from my grandmother in her passing.

As I stood at the lectern reading her eulogy I reflected on the support she had given me throughout my life; especially at the age of 16 when I ran away from home and moved interstate with my (later to be) husband.

At her funeral I read about a time in her life when she was 16 years old when the war broke out in

Holland. I realised in that moment standing at the lectern, looking at the weeping faces of my family that every one of us has a unique story to tell.

And every one of us has the opportunity to have a rich and long life.

I realised I wanted my life to be as rich and long as possible.

This realisation struck me - I was a far different woman than I was just 6 months previously. 6 months ago I was at a point in my life where I actually understood why people could commit suicide because of my own crippling anxiety and was almost resigned to living out the rest of my days in a boring predictable future and passionless marriage.

I decided, in that moment reading her eulogy that I wanted my eulogy to be inspiring and to leave a rich legacy in the world.

That weekend I wrote my own eulogy.

It was an eye opening process.

The main realisation I had writing my eulogy was that I have so much time.

I have time to start a business. I have time to write many, many books!

I have time to travel the world. I have time to live in Bali. I have time to study piano. I have time to learn yoga.

I have time for it all!

This realisation coupled with the dissatisfaction with my work spurred me to start getting skills to add to my tool-belt to 'connect people to their souls.'

My spiritual awakening called to me. I spent a lot of time visualising my dream life and dream job — it seemed a little crazy, even to me.

Although my logical mind wanted to know HOW to make this all happen, some part of me just told myself to take one step at a time.

So, I decided I better start investing in myself and set out to get some credentials.

I realised I could better use my six-figure salary (while it lasted) to up-skill as quickly as possible to build my dream job. To build my dream life. This was my chance and I was ready!

I wrote out my ideal dream job and working conditions.

'I work 3-4 hours a day, I swim in the ocean every day. I help people live their best lives. I teach

people strategies to improve their lives. I am healthy. I am vibrant. I am inspiring.'

It didn't seem like a 'job' and it certainly didn't seem 'realistic' at the time!

****

Yes, the 'dream job' I wrote out a few years ago seemed completely unrealistic. But that paragraph is an exact summary of a typical day in my life these days. The only difference is, my life is even better than I imagined!

I think a lot of people are waiting for their 'dream job offer' without realising that we have to give it to ourselves.

You can design your dream life yourself!

You have to give yourself permission to dream.

You have to build and exercise your dreaming muscles.

Do you allow yourself the pleasurable experience of sitting and day-dreaming about all of the many various possibilities in the future?

If you don't, then you are likely suffering from weak dreaming muscles.

If you have weak dreaming muscles and you get an idea about the future, your weak dreaming muscles will just look at all the ways it won't work.

What about if you have a weak, tiny dream and something happens in your life, like a financial down-turn or a relationship break up?

Or you tell someone about your dreams and they shut them down because they sound crazy?

That's right, the dream will shrivel up because you weren't strong enough to protect it!

If you don't exercise your dreaming muscles then how are you going to know which dream is the dream you want to follow?

If you haven't given yourself enough time to imagine your dream becoming a reality how can you decide if you even really want that reality?

The last thing you want to do is jump from one dream to the next until you have had time to consider if it's the right thing to pursue.

So, let's do some dreaming exercises together…

Process 1: Exercise Your Dreaming Muscles

Imagine for a moment you are a millionaire.

Imagine waking up in your big comfortable bed after a deep night's sleep.

You yawn, stretch, and step out of bed. Imagine what kind of house you are living in as this millionaire version of you.

Imagine the clothes you would wear. Imagine the breakfast you would eat. Even imagine the car you drive.

Imagine the kind of job you have (if you even work at all!).

Most of all I want you to imagine how it would feel to wake up and live this life.

It feels nice doesn't it?

It may feel expansive, it may feel exhilarating, it may feel abundant.

Write down the words that come to mind for you about how it feels to dream and imagine this million dollar version of you:

I felt _____

I saw _____

I smelled _____

I heard _____

I _____

If you take away nothing from reading this book than just allowing yourself the gift of dreaming more and imagining being a millionaire more often, your life will change— dramatically.

Why is this?

Studies have now proven that the power of visualisation has very similar neurological effects as if the body is actually experiencing it.

The mind makes it real.

Psychology Today published an article in 2009 which looked into a study about brain patterns in weight-lifters and found that the patterns activated when a weightlifter lifted hundreds of pounds were similarly activated when they only imagined lifting.

Why am I telling you this?

In my work so much of what I do with my clients is visualisation.

Visualisation helps form the neural pathways to make dreams a reality, and allow the dreams into our life. It allows us to get more comfortable with living the idea of a dream. It's a magical map for the journey.

On my journey of relaunching my life **I imagined the exact life I am living now.**

I imagined living in a bright light filled home, wearing yoga gear, working with people around the world and feeling deeply fulfilled in a loving and passionate relationship.

Four years ago I was living a VERY different life.

I was still married to my ex-husband. I was in debt. I was living on alcohol, chocolate and caffeine and suffering anxiety, and I was feeling stressed sitting at a dimly lit computer with a stiff back every single day in my job. I had absolutely zero idea HOW I would get to this life I am living today or that it was even a possibility.

But, the steps that I am explaining to you in this book are what I did to get here, the rest, was left to the universe.

In fact, I did less and imagined more.

The less I pushed, the more I received.

I believe now that we don't make our dreams happen — we let our dreams happen.

But we have to invest the time to *imagine* what those dreams are in order to allow them to manifest into reality.

So, take a few minutes right now to close your eyes and visualise your ideal day.

What would it look like, what would it feel like, what would you do and how would you spend the day, from start to finish?

Take your time with this and close your eyes, breath calmly (perhaps with a smile on your face) and imagine it for a few minutes.

Write down what you imagined:

_____

_____

_____

Process 2: Dream Drawing

Another excellent way to exercise your dreaming muscles is to allow yourself to dream using your right brain instead of your left.

One morning a few months before I started my business I sketched a picture of the mandala and wording of my company logo whilst taking a train into work.

I didn't know it at the time, and there were lots of doodles and drawings that didn't make any sense but I will never forget seeing my company logo, and realising it was exactly what I had drawn months earlier, when the concept was nothing more than a dream.

How can you do this?

Firstly, ensure you have some time alone.

Take a piece of paper and some coloured pencils and markers and put some beautiful music on.

Light a candle and allow yourself to write the word 'DREAMS' on a piece of blank paper and simply allow your soul to fall out onto the paper.

Draw whatever comes out of you, without judgement. Keep this paper and repeat this step as often as possible.

Process 3: Avoid Dream Crushers

Ask yourself, who is a 'Dream Crusher' in your life at the moment?

Note: Dream Crushers often mean well, but they are ultimately shutting down your dreams before they have grown strong enough to fly.

From my experience, people shut down other people's dreams for two reasons.

First, they are trying to protect you from failing. This is something all animals do for protection. If one animal is running outside of the flock, the rest of the colony will try to herd them back into line for safety.

The second, is they are unconsciously jealous. There is a part of all of us that wants to pursue our dreams. But so few of us actually do so. When someone hears someone sharing a wonderful dream (if they are not pursuing their own) they can unintentionally shut it down to make themselves feel better for not pursuing their own dreams.

Most dream crushers have just had their dreams crushed too… perhaps a very long time ago.

I honestly believe that **jealousy is just inspiration in disguise!**

So, send them love, and inspire them with your ability to grow your dreaming muscles.

Let your success and happiness show them that it's never too late for them to relaunch their lives too!

Once your dreaming muscles are strong and producing results they will see the success in you and soon step aside.

And once you truly know yourself, your values, your dreams and your hopes then you will know which dreams to pursue.

If you find yourself reading this book thinking *'But I don't KNOW what I want to do yet!'* or *'I don't have a dream'* then that's okay. Just read on, and trust that something will bubble up and surface when the time is right.

Note: sometimes we are our own dream crushers! By default, if you are not allowing yourself to dream then you are crushing your dreams before they even get to see the light of day. Follow the activity at the end of this chapter and allow yourself to dream.

I highly suggest keeping a blank notepad handy for ideas and just collate them as you go. Rome wasn't built in a day... piece by piece, the jigsaw puzzle of your life will come together.

When your dreams are ready and they feel right you will know. If you are in tune with your feelings and emotions, rather than orchestrating how you feel things should be.

Remember, if you feel crazy doing these processes, that's okay! I have a favourite saying 'I would rather be crazy and happy than sane and miserable!' Sometimes we have to step outside the known to create the future we want.

Before I ask you to reflect and take some notes, it's also important to realise that sometimes we will hear the voice of a dream crusher like a tape deck in our own mind.

So, dream crushers can also be that teacher in primary school who told you that you weren't smart enough, your mother who told you that you shouldn't get too smart or men will be intimidated *(a lot of girls heard this one!)* or your first boyfriend who broke your heart.

These dream crushers can hold us back even if they aren't in our lives any more.

Who are the dream crushers in your life (past or present), and how can you avoid taking on their doubts and fears?

_____

_____

_____

I first met Angela in August 2015 at a Yoga Course in Ubud, Bali.

She was a polite Swiss girl with deep brown eyes who seemed quite shy at first.

At lunch, we started chatting and her eyes lit up when I told her how I had changed my life in the past year and was now living a life of my own design. She asked me to help her.

She admitted she was miserable back home in Switzerland. She told me she felt she was stuck in a nine-to-five-hamster wheel, running to her corporate job, part-time studying, family and friends, some sports, flat and all over again.

She was single and deep within longing to live a more meaningful and conscious life alongside her partner and eventually a family. But her lifestyle left her exhausted with less space and no energy to pursue any of her passions.

I asked her why she didn't just stop her studies and immediately the light in her eyes vanished. She told me it's what her parents would have wanted for her. A safe, successful job. She asked me to coach her and help her find fulfilment just like she saw in me.

In her first session, overlooking the rice fields in Ubud I helped her release her ties to her parents, create her own set boundaries and to take control of her own life. To stop living as a result of the obligations and expectations of others.

I helped her connect to her soul purpose, and allowed her to realise she wanted to experience more in this world than just sitting in an office all *day, every day. She visualised herself travelling the world, and living in Bali one day, and thought this looked impossible at the time.*

After six months of working together, she quit her job, gave up the lease on her flat in Switzerland and bought a one way ticket to Bali, where she is still living today.

When I saw her on my last trip to Bali she looked like a completely different woman.

Alive, vibrant and free.

For me, it is a soul filling joy to see people living life to their fullest potential; and to see that scared, yet excited glint in their eyes of a life lived fully!

On the back of a scooter with Angela in
October 2016 in Bali

KEY TAKE-AWAYS

- Visualisation is a powerful tool to use as often as you can
- Get creative and explore your dreams without judgement
- Avoid sharing your dreams with dream crushers until they are well formed

ACTIVITY

Write your eulogy (include your age when you die, how many children and grandchildren you have (if any), and the things you experienced and achieved in your whole entire life).

CHAPTER 8

_____

_____

_____

_____

_____

_____

_____

_____

Rediscover the Magic Within

'Those who don't believe in magic will never find it.'
– Roald Dahl

A few months after my grandmother passed away, I met my soul-mate.

Believe it or not, I found him as a result of a psychic reading!

If I didn't have the recorded evidence of the reading she gave me, I wouldn't even believe it myself.

She told me his name and she told me how it would feel when we met, that there would be a *knowing*.

She told me he was a teacher and we would travel the world together teaching the world things to improve their lives.

She told me in the reading 'Honey, your guides keep yelling at me "Where is Paul?" 'I told her I didn't know anyone called Paul.

I know this part of my story sounds absolutely crazy. I was highly sceptical but when I met Paul a few weeks later, I knew she was right.

The only way I can describe what it was like to meet Paul was it felt like I had arrived home.

If you can imagine the feeling you get when you finally arrive home after months and months of travelling and fall asleep in your own bed in freshly washed sheets.

That's what it felt like in his presence.

I felt like I could finally stop and relax.

He is the most incredible man I have ever met in my entire life, my best friend, my soul-mate and his very existence has made me believe in miracles. I know that if I brought him into my life, I can do anything.

His existence turned the sceptical and logical side of me into a believer of all things mystical and unseen.

He is beyond what I thought was possible to manifest in a partner.

I am thankful everyday for having him by my side and life has never, ever felt the same.

We have fun, passion, purpose and we make a difference together.

I never believed in the concept of soul-mates until the day I met Paul.

*With Paul after a Cirque du Soleil
show in Las Vegas in 2016*

This experience opened my belief structure so wide that I started opening more to my spirituality.

I deepened my connection to my intuition and things started to fall in place. I started to learn more about the power of belief of the human mind and how to wield it in ways that were empowering and magical.

I also played with the idea that if I can have a soul-mate connection so intense, then past lives must exist.

I delved into different forms of therapy and healing, and had some profound experiences with past life regressions and energy healing.

I rediscovered the magic that had been dormant within me for so long. I had unexplainable experiences and felt like life would never be the same again. All of a sudden my black and white corporate life was thrust into a 3D multicolour miracle one day after the next.

The more I uncovered this side of myself, trusted my intuition and paired it with my dreams the more my life started to weave into shape.

I became qualified in Hypnotherapy Certification, NLP Practitioner Training, Reiki I, II and Masters and Heartmath™ Resiliency coaching and felt at home.

These modalities resonated with my soul and I suddenly had skills to help people overcome all the mental and emotional problems that were holding them back!

I was inspired to register a business name immediately and start coaching clients on Saturdays. There was no hesitation in taking the first step. It felt right in my entire being.

As news spread about my business and qualifications, colleagues at work started admitting to me that they struggled with anxiety and booked in appointments to see me after hours. In the beginning I only charged $50 per session for 'relaxation hypnosis sessions', which barely covered my costs for room hire. But, I didn't care!

I was making a difference, and the results my clients got gave me a deep sense of fulfilment.

As my eyes opened to a new world around me my office job started paling in comparison.

My Saturday coaching and hypnosis appointments started filling as word of mouth started to spread. One colleague who was stressed and miserable before our session literally floated back into work the Monday morning after our coaching session and I had 5 colleagues book in with me as a result of her shift.

My client's results were my advertising.

I truly believed in my clients being able to redesign ANY aspect of their life. It was this belief that I projected onto my clients and their results shifted.

The clients I have worked with over the last few years have met soul mates, quit jobs, started new businesses, lost weight, resolved anxiety and healed relationships.

As demand increased, I negotiated to reduce my hours at work to 4 days a week so that I was able to spend more time building my business.

At times I felt nervous and even questioned if I was ruining my corporate career, but the way I felt when I was working in my own business told me it was the right decision.

My entire being felt at peace when I was in my zone of genius and although I was in very new terrain, I felt safely guided by something larger than me.

It felt incredible to finally be answering the call I had received many months ago when I first spoke to my soul.

So many changes, so many decisions, so much courage.

But it was all worth it to be finally doing what made my soul feel alive...

****

Our intuition is something we are born with.

But, it is something a lot of us 'talk' ourselves out of trusting. At the time I visited the psychic, I didn't have a strong connection with my intuition at all.

Despite the fact that I had started on this journey of self-discovery, I was still a long way from having a connection with my inner truth.

I was still relying on my 'logical mind' and asking other people to help me make sense of this world. Something I now realise is not always possible!

There are unexplainable things in this world.

The science world tries so hard to explain the magic out of everything, but it is far off in my view based on the experiences I have had. Some things are just not meant to be understood by our logical brains.

Since I started trusting in the beautiful wisdom of the unknown my life has unravelled into a magical tapestry of experiences I could never have planned myself.

I am a Reiki, Karuna and Seichim Master and hold a Bachelor of Metaphysics and Diploma of Neuro-psychological Immunology. I have also studied Shamanism and Tantra as a means of not only helping ourselves connect to our higher self, but also as a means of strengthening and reconnecting to our intuition.

What I love most about Reiki is that Science cannot yet prove how it works, and yet there are more Reiki practitioners in the world than there are doctors, and there are now over 800+ (and counting!) hospitals in America that offer Reiki as a complementary form of treatment to cancer patients.

This is truly empowering because we live in a society where most solutions are 'external' in the form of a drug or a professional.

I believe that when we go within, and connect to our spiritual or higher selves we find the answers to everything. We can stop getting the answers 'out there' and start finding the solutions inside.

The other wonderful thing about energy and intention healing, is that it empowers us to know that we can facilitate our own self-healing, and that we do not need to seek healing through or from other people.

When we look at healing ourselves from a metaphysical perspective, we focus on working with all four of our energy bodies.

Different resources refer to many more energy bodies, however, I have chosen to keep this concept simple for the purpose of this book.

The main four energy bodies are:

- physical
- emotional
- mental
- spiritual

Our physical energy body is our most dense and heaviest of the energy bodies and this is where dis-ease resides. This is where most modern medicine focuses.

Therefore, in order to experience dis-ease in the physical body this 'dis-ease' or 'dis-harmony' has to have travelled through the other three energy bodies first.

So, in other words, before we experience physical symptoms, the dis-ease must have come through us emotionally, mentally and spiritually.

I believe the more connected we are to our spiritual body then the more likely we are to prevent negative illness or disharmony from cascading down into the emotional, mental and physical bodies.

The body can be an extremely useful tool for understanding what is going on beneath the surface. So I encourage you to start exploring this and getting curious about what your body may be trying to tell you.

There are some great books on this if you haven't come across this concept before which I have listed at the back of this book in the Resources section.

In my classes I also encourage students to develop their intuition. We do this with a number of tools, namely through practice card reading and learning about how to feel intuitive 'yes' and 'no's' in their physical body.

You can try this right now.

Activity:

Take a deep breath and close your eyes.

Then say the word **YES** to yourself out loud as loud as possible and get a 'sense' for where these words come from, and how your body responds.

Then say the word **NO** and notice how your body and cells respond, and where this word impacts your body in the strongest way.

Personally, to me, a YES feels like an uplifting and energising feeling in my heart and chest. I feel my shoulders draw back and down and I feel light and visualise white in my entire upper torso.

A NO on the other hand feels heavy, tight and almost nauseous in my gut. I sense a dark colour energetically and feel heavy in my stomach.

I base a lot of my decisions on asking myself questions and feeling into my body's response.

This has become sharper as I've developed my connection and removed surface level emotions such as anxiety and stress that can block intuition.

Chakras

Whilst I am not going to go in-depth about Chakras in this book I would encourage you to explore this system as it is an ancient method for understanding our blockages, emotions and ailments.

Basically, the term chakra translates to 'wheel' in Sanskrit and in our energy body we have wheels or vortexes of energy.

There are hundreds of chakra points, but the main seven chakras are the most studied as they correspond with a different gland of the body and if blocked can display different symptoms (e.g. the throat chakra aligns with the thyroid and relates to self expression, creativity and alignment with our chosen vocation).

Chakras

Crown (PINEAL GLAND)

Third Eye (PITUITARY GLAND)

Throat (THYROID)

Heart (THYMUS)

Solar Plexus (PANCREAS)

Sacral Chakra (SEX GLANDS)

Root (ADRENALS)

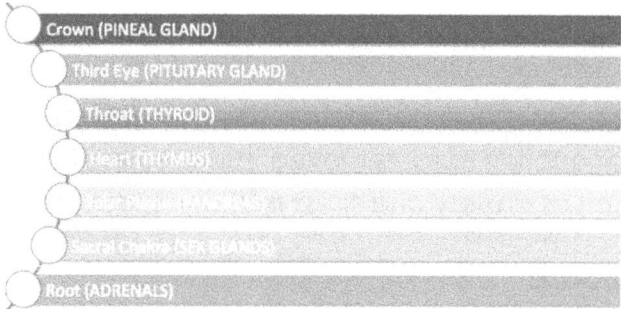

To live your most fulfilling life then you need to have a strong connection with your intuition. And this involves connecting with all four of your energy bodies, not just working on yourself physically but mentally, emotionally and spiritually too.

Because your intuition is the part of you that knows when to hold onto the handle-bars of this rollercoaster called life and it is also the part of you that knows to fasten your seat-belt.

Your intuition will ground you, hold you steady and make you feel confident about your decisions. I believe that our intuition is our best teacher. It's the true teacher within.

It's within you, and if you don't trust it yet, then you just need to develop it.

Here are some further steps to help you develop your intuition:

Process 1: Learn to Receive

The first thing you need to do to receive from your intuition is to clear the trash in your mind and body.

If your head is full of mindless chatter and fears and it hasn't been cleared out recently then the signal from your intuition won't be as strong as it can be.

Notice which energy or vibration lowering activities you have partaken in; such as gossip, junk food, television and fear. Instead start to practice raising your energetic quality through practicing gratitude, consuming organic food, monitoring your thoughts and drinking good quality water.

A regular meditation practice, journaling routine, yoga practice and self-healing with Reiki is a powerful way to clear the junk in your mind.

This one's up to you, and no one else can do this work for you.

I have had situations where during a meditation I have received specific answers to a life situation that I wasn't conscious of prior to the meditation.

Now my intuition is very clear, and very strong. I use it as a compass in my life, and it also assists me with my work with clients.

It's a powerful tool to have a strong connection to the teacher within you.

If you want a strong connection with your intuition then you need to start making time for you. Time to clear out the trash in your mind so that you can receive clear messages and signs.

Process 2: Learn to Trust

What is beautiful about your intuition is that it got you here.

You are reading this book because of your intuition.

If you doubted your intuition you would have never picked up this book. Even if you're reading this book because a friend gave it to you, then you have still created that situation to read these words out of everything else you could be conscious of right now.

So, the same feeling or sense you had about deciding to read this book and not watch TV instead is the exact same feeling or sense that your intuition gets when something is right for you.

Follow the feeling that led you to reading this book.

If you do, your intuition will continue to lead you to more clues on the quest of your life.

Sometimes, you don't want to listen to your intuition about something in your life because it frightens you.

One of my clients Rachael was scared to admit that she didn't want her job anymore, because she didn't value herself enough to find another job or start her business. She had also recently ended a long-term relationship so felt very afraid and vulnerable.

But slowly, slowly, step-by-step, together we peeled back the layers of her low self-confidence and started helping her feel more empowered. As we worked together she started seeing her own light and trusting it and owning it. Now she has a new job in an industry that matches her values and has started running her own workshops empowering women to love themselves and build confidence in their lives.

Life unfolds one step at a time. And the more you build your dreaming and intuition muscles the easier and more confident you become each step of the way.

The way I see it, you want to have your eyes gently gazing on the horizon but the rest of your being firmly present to the moment and taking it all one step at a time.

Process 3: Deepen the Connection

I've spoken about how important it is to know where you are right now when relaunching your life, but it is also vitally important to know where you have come from.

Why?

In the chapter 'Everyone and Everything is a Mirror', I will introduce you to the idea that everyone in your life is there to teach you something.

It's a pretty powerful realisation if you truly embrace it and apply it as a philosophy in your life.

Out of all of the teachers you may come across in the stages of your life, who is the one constant teacher?

It's YOU.

Imagine for a moment, you are standing on stage at a theatre in front of an audience.

Now, imagine sitting in the audience watching yourself standing on stage.

Let's look at this character, called you.

You are the number one biggest teacher in your life!

In life, we either learn from the mistakes we make or we continue to repeat them.

Once we have learned a lesson, there is no need for it to repeat again in our life (unless we actually didn't learn from it in the first place!).

So, have you truly taken the time to reflect deeply on your life and your life lessons?

Wouldn't it be powerful to be able to reflect on your life, in order to calculate what lessons you still need to overcome in your future?

If you ignore this aspect of yourself, you are essentially flying blind into your future.

You want to take time to reflect on the past before journeying further into your future as it will help you understand, appreciate and honour your authentic self.

This chapter is powerful in helping you to understand the nuts and bolts of how your life works.

It's like understanding the safety locks and mechanisms of the actual ride of life which helps you know what is keeping you safe.

So let's explore the decisions and experiences you have had in life and what they have taught you.

ACTIVITY

What is one of the best decisions you have ever made in your life?

_____

_____

_____

Why was this such a powerful decision for you, and what did it teach you?

_____

_____

_____

Great, now let's look at the other side.

One of the absolute worst decisions of my life was basing my career choices on what my head told me to do, instead of listening to what my heart wanted!

When I listened to other people instead of myself.

Climbing the corporate ladder was definitely not

my life's purpose. But it's what I thought I should do. And I was so cut off from my intuition that I ignored all the signs.

Each time I was promoted I felt a little more trapped, each pay-rise and additional expectation was like a noose tightening that little bit more.

This not so positive decision, taught me the power in listening to my heart and intuition.

In hindsight, it is reassuring to now know that I will not do what my head/logic/society encourages because I am in tune with my heart, it would be next to impossible for me to ignore it.

ACTIVITY

What is one of the worst decisions you have made in your life?

_____

_____

_____

Why was this such a bad decision, and what did it teach you?

_____

_____

_____

Great, now let's expand on this.

For the worst decision, can you recognise what signs your intuition tried to give you to warn you about your decision along the way?

_____

_____

_____

When did you first decide to ignore your intuition and listen to logic instead?

_____

_____

_____

Make a promise to yourself to give yourself enough stillness and silence to allow your intuition to speak to you, so that you can avoid costly mistakes in the future that you can potentially prevent.

One final thought is that our intuition can be impacted or blocked around how we are managing our hormones.

From the age of 15 to the age of 26 I took a daily high dose contraceptive pill, like a lot of women my age do.

For 11 years I did not know what it was like to feel my own natural hormones and experience a natural connection to myself as a woman.

When I finally went off the pill in early 2013, it was less than a year later that I started reconnecting to my intuition (or true self) and thus continued to make decisions from then on that changed my life for the better. It's almost as if I finally was myself after over a decade of living on synthetic hormones that blocked my intuition and feminine wisdom.

I encourage you to look at any synthetic chemicals or medications you are taking and simply consider how they may be impacting your natural sense of self and speak to a professional about your options.

I am not suggesting you take yourself off any medications but I certainly encourage you to seek a second opinion to be as informed as you can about your choices.

Our bodies are impacted by our endocrine systems and I have personally found a much deeper sense of connection to myself since removing all medications and state-altering substances.

Please note: I can't prove that the contraceptive pill blocked my intuition, but it makes sense to me personally from my own experience.

IMPORTANCE OF RITUALS

I believe rituals are a missing element in our Western society.

I travel to Bali at least 2 times a year and I love seeing the locals placing their offerings around their homes, cars, scooters and workplaces as a sign of gratitude to the Gods.

One way I love to connect to the magic inside, through rituals, is through the use of guidance cards.

Each morning I perform a simple practice that centres me before yoga and meditation which is to spend a few moments in reflection at my altar (a space in my home adorned with crystals, candles and a Ganesh and Buddha statue).

I select a guidance card for the day and whilst I don't live and die by the message in the card, it is interesting to reflect upon the keys, clues and messages within it. I also reflect upon the message once more before going to bed in the evening.

Paul and I also have a ritual of sharing three things we are grateful for morning and night, and we never get out of bed until we can say 'we are going to have an amazing day today!'.

An example of a simple altar at home

I believe that rituals are incredibly important, especially for women who have lost this practice in the modern era. Often women do instinctively perform rituals such as spring cleaning the house, only to find out later that it's a new moon, or let go of things we no longer need, only to later realise it is the full moon.

I am always surprised how few people I work with have a ritual, and after I suggest it to them, they report back to me on how it makes them feel centred and grounded.

By adding a small ceremony into their lives my clients have replaced irrational fears, bad habits and addictions and even reduced stress. The overall feedback is always that they feel more centred and grounded by spending this time on themselves in quiet contemplation.

Urban Shaman, Donna Henes is a ritual expert and guest author for *The Huffington Post* considers rituals as important as our needs for food, shelter and love.

She states that 'When we set aside the quality time and claim the psychic space for ceremony, when we assume the authority to do so, we are able to transform our perceptions, our perspectives, our experiences, and in the process, our reality.'

Another example of a ritual you may like to perform, aside from the one I have suggested above is to draw an outline of your experiences in your journal as you come to the end of each month.

In this way you reflect upon your achievements, successes and memories which can help you to become more conscious of your life and what you are creating.

ACTIVITY

What rituals do you currently have in your life? Where could you add a dimension of magic, reflection and ceremony into your world?

_____

_____

_____

KEY TAKE-AWAYS

- To connect to your intuition, clear your mind through meditation or journaling.
- Review the best and worst decisions of your life and notice how you ignored your intuition when it turned out negative.
- Consider starting a daily or weekly ritual and building an altar for reflection.

CHAPTER 9

Everything and Everyone
is a Mirror

'The world around us is nothing more and nothing less than a mirror of what we have become from within.' – Gregg Braden

In late 2014 I travelled alone to Mexico, Puerto Vallarta to attend a conference called 'Awesomeness Fest.'

This event offers 350 selected global entrepreneurs from over 1500 applicants who want to make a difference in the world the opportunity to mingle and attend self-development talks over a five-day period.

The moment I heard about the event I decided I was going.

I wasn't surprised when I was selected. *It was as though the event had been designed for me.*

Travelling to Mexico on my own was a huge thrill!

On my way to Mexico I stayed over a few nights in Hollywood. I made friends in my hostel off Hollywood Blvd with a beautiful Swedish woman named Argavan. She was a published author with big dreams to empower Iranian women to find their voices and we both talked about our ideas to change the world. She told me I MUST write a book, and soon. I promised her I would.

At Awesomeness Fest I felt like a free spirit who had found her place. I met as many people as I could over the five days, including Vishen Lakhiani (founder of Mindvalley), comedian Kyle Cease, motivational speaker Lisa Nicholls and Emily Fletcher (founder of Ziva Meditation).

With Vishen Lakhiani, Founder of
Mindvalley in November 2014.

Spending a week with inspiring and encouraging entrepreneurs from all around the world was life-changing, not only for my confidence but in what I believed was possible for myself.

As one of only four other Australians at the conference, I became well known and people approached me throughout the week to 'talk to the inspiring Aussie girl.'

I had CEOs of multinational organisations from France, Canada and America look me in the eye and tell me they believed in me and my vision and that I was special.

As a result, my vision for my future turned worldwide.

On the final evening of the Awesomeness Fest, a yacht took us to a mystery island for dinner and on the way, I started chatting to a friendly American businessman.

We talked at the back of the yacht overlooking the sunset over the ocean for over an hour and I shared my vision for the future and my business with him.

He gave me some advice and at the end of the conversation he said, "It was a real pleasure speaking to you Juliet. I can tell you're going to be a success. I can see it in your eyes when you talk. Not everyone has that sparkle — your soul is truly alive when you talk about your dreams!"

How different this conversation was to the one I had during my wake up call just two years earlier on the back of a different sailing boat!

Now I was on the back of a sailing boat again but this time I had a successful businessman telling me that he believed in me. I realised I was a very different woman to the one two years prior. My dreams were alive, I was brave, I was finally on my path.

A lot can change in a few years.

****

I love to imagine that life is a game. Imagine that it's a video game and that your character has been loaded.

And in this game, you have a quest.

Your quest is to find your purpose and live your most fulfilling life.

There are three things that will help you in this quest of your life:

1. Teachers
2. Classes
3. Clues

1) Teachers

Imagine for a moment that everyone in your life is a teacher.

Everyone!

Myself, your Mum, your pet, your boss at work, your life partner, your child, the man sitting at the bus stop.

In this interactive video game, all of these teachers have a role to play in your life.

Some of these teachers are here to guide you the right way. You generally get points in the form of positive emotion when you are around these teachers.

Some teachers are here to show you which way not to go. You generally feel negative emotion around these teachers.

Some teachers are here to remind you about the ways you went wrong in the past and some teachers are here to show you truths about yourself you do not want to admit.

These last two teachers are usually the people who trigger you the most. These are the ones you can have a tendency to blame, or judge.

But these teachers are just as powerful as the others (if not more so!).

On the quest of your life, if you see everyone in your life as a teacher, life gets more interesting.

You can start to ponder, **why do I have this particular teacher in my life?**

Or what is this person trying to teach me?

I often remind my clients that *nothing goes away until we have learned what we need to.*

Even if they leave their workplace, if they haven't learned from all the people there, then they will attract those types of people again perhaps in the next workplace or at some point later in life.

If you were in a video game, you can't progress to the next level until you have defeated the 'boss.' It's the same in life.

Learn from the teachers around you and move forward. Try to avoid or blame them and you will get them again and again in different forms.

ACTIVITY

Take a moment to write out five of the biggest teachers in your life to date. It can be anyone.

Perhaps pick one person you love and feel happy around, one person who triggers you, and three other big teachers (positive or negative) from your life's quest so far.

_____

_____

_____

_____

Now, take a moment to think about three things about each person.

1. What do they do that you admire?

   _____

   _____

   _____

2. What do they do that you don't like?

   _____

   _____

   _____

3. Why are they in your life, what have you learned from them?

   _____

   _____

   _____

Remember, some people are here in our lives to show us how not to be!

What did you notice?

Could you imagine how different your life would have been if these teachers weren't in it?

How powerful is that to realise? Perhaps you can even be thankful for them.

I encourage you to expand this list.

I ask my clients to do this exercise for the 20 biggest teachers in their lives and it is always incredibly eye-opening.

The last step in this exercise is to thank all of the teachers in your life.

How else would you learn all of the things that you know, if they didn't teach them to you?

It's up to you to identify and realise the lessons.

If you keep avoiding the same type of teachers, you will attract more and more of them in different personas.

Once you learn what you need to, generally that teacher will move on (or stop having to teach you that lesson).

Sometimes the lesson is that you need to stand up to a teacher, to tell them what you won't accept from them anymore.

Sometimes it's to express your truth to them.

Sometimes it's to overcome jealousy.

Sometimes it's to learn to be patient.

And sometimes it's to learn to love yourself more.

There is always a reason someone is in your life.

Once you understand the lessons that teachers bring to you, you can see them as guides in your life. Because some people are here to reflect parts of us back to ourselves.

So, use their assistance as best as you can – both the positive and the negative.

Forgive, thank and release the teachers in your lives and miraculous things will occur.

One way to do this is through the use of a healing prayer.

I personally have experienced people's demeanour completely change, *if I simply think about* the following prayer in my mind when I am in their presence. They can go from angry and upset to calm and relaxed in a matter of seconds. It really is that powerful. Try it yourself.

Activity

This is the Ho'oponopono Hawaiian healing prayer.

Place your hand on your heart and say the following prayer aloud (in any order) at least three times.

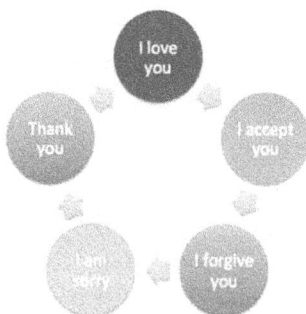

Ho'oponopono Prayer

I love you

I accept you

I forgive you

I am sorry

Thank you

Next, practice thinking of one of the listed teachers in your life and reciting the Ho'oponopono Hawaiian healing prayer whilst thinking of them.

Do this as often as necessary to release negative thoughts and energy towards anyone in your life.

I encourage you to choose people you have the strongest negative charge to. They have been your most powerful teachers, and deserve the most gratitude for playing this powerful teaching role in your life.

2) Classes

In the quest of your life, if you have teachers then you would presume that you have to also attend classes, right?

Still in the video game - classes are the patterns (or categories) of experiences you are having in your life. The themes, if you will.

One night I was driving home from work shortly after starting my business Relaunch My Life and I crashed my car into the back of a taxi.

It was a small crash, and luckily no one was hurt but at the time I looked up to the sky and said 'yes universe, I know I need to slow down!'

The very next day I was reversing my car out of a car-park in a supermarket and I crashed the side door into a cement pole.

The very next day.

Two crashes in 24 hours!

Again, I looked up at the sky and said 'I know... I still didn't slow down did I? Sorry...'

When I physically look up at the sky I still don't know if it's to the universe, to my guides, to my higher self, or to my angels, or even past ancestors who may be looking out for me.

I try not to label things too much. I believe we all have our own belief structures and for me, I know there is someone or something watching over me and guiding me. Now, rather than trying to prove or define it, I simply trust and connect with that source as a constant way of life.

Luckily these were just superficial crashes, no one was injured and I took the lesson. I realised that I was being shown that I needed to 'slow down' not just in my driving - but in my life, or I could get hurt.

After the second accident - I actually listened!

I slowed down.

It is not always easy to notice the patterns, but it is so fun when you have that light-bulb moment and certain themes or patterns come up in your life, because then you can do something about it!

Activity

Think about any negative experiences you are having at the moment and notice if there are any parallels in your life in any other areas.

For example, family dynamics / work/ relationship – become aware of any patterns of how you handle situations or conversations.

Are you going too fast (having accidents) or going too slow (getting parking fines)?

Are you hearing the same conversations over and over in different people?

Are you feeling similar emotions on a daily basis in different situations?

Take time to notice patterns, because they are there to help you 'course correct,' and once corrected you will begin to feel more stable in your daily life.

3) Clues

In your life's quest, aside from teachers to learn from and classes to attend to, there is one more element to help you grow and expand and 'go to the next level. The fun part — finding clues!

You may have heard the saying, the universe leaves clues.

I'm here to tell you – it most certainly does!

The only catch is, it's up to you to notice them.

These can be in the form of a street sign with a name of an ex-partner or old friend.

They can be links between friends that help you know you are on the right path.

An example could be when you meet a few people with the same name in the space of a week or two.

Or you see the same numbers or words over and over.

Or everyone starts talking about a course you've never heard of before.

Consider the meaning, what this evokes in you and what it could be teaching you.

Learn to listen in more ways than one. Get curious.

I believe that our external world reflects our internal world, and so noting what is happening and the people you are attracting in your life is a powerful clue to a flourishing life.

ACTIVITY

Your activity for this entire section is to notice the clues the universe gives you in the next 24 hours, and their potential meanings.

Clue: _____

Meaning:_____

Clue: _____

Meaning:_____

KEY TAKE-AWAYS

- See everyone in your life as your teacher or a mirror (or both)
- Notice the patterns occurring in your life
- Keep your eyes open for clues provided by the universe on your path.

CHAPTER 10

Fear is an Illusion

'Everything you want is on the other side of fear.'
– Jack Canfield

The day after I arrived back in Australia from Mexico I resigned from my full-time job.

Everyone thought I was crazy.

I wondered if I was too!

If I stayed at work *for just another 5 months* I would be eligible for pro-rata long service leave.

That would have been a five-figure payout!

But I honestly could not sell my soul for another day.

I decided I would rather be crazy and happy than sane and miserable.

I felt so undervalued, unfulfilled and unappreciated at my office job. And when I worked with my coaching clients I felt a deep sense of peace and fulfilment.

Nothing could compare.

Towards the end, the worse I felt at work the easier the decision became.

I was frightened about the future but I trusted that it was the right step in my journey. Paul encouraged me and would tell me to 'just quit!' as often as possible.

I knew somehow that my courage would be rewarded, as it had seemed to be thus far.

So on the 18th of November 2014 I resigned from my job and faced my future head on.

I had to serve a long, and drawn out 4 week notice period.

About two weeks in I asked myself 'So, I'm still here … what is there still for me to learn?'

I realised I needed to have an honest conversation with the Senior Managers before I left, to answer some unanswered questions about their decisions.

This conversation was enlightening for me and it taught me to speak up, to understand all perspectives in a situation and question the status quo and also my own belief system.

I firmly believe that having this difficult conversation before I left taught me how to have difficult conversations and saved me the need to learn this in my business later on.

I walked away from my six-figure salary with a one week annual leave payout, 5 months before my long service leave period would have been reached.

The day I resigned from my job.

On my last day, I packed my belongings and said goodbye to the colleagues at workplace that had been my second home since I was 21 years old.

I stepped out into the world, vulnerable, with an infant of a business and a heart full of hope.

In less than 12 months I left my husband and my job, started a business, had a death in the family and moved house twice. In the 'life stress measurement scales' I was high risk. But I had never felt better.

I hired a full-time office space in a women's entrepreneurial co-working hub and I created the space for my success to find me. The environment was a hive of entrepreneurial activity and the woman hiring the office next to me a bubbly woman named Taryn Brumfitt. She told me she was working on a documentary on healing women's body image called 'Embrace'. Something told me she was going to change the world.

Yes, surrounded by women like her, I knew I was definitely in the right place.

Four weeks after leaving, I became so busy with clients I was earning the same money as my six-figure salary and working half as much! Plus I was doing what made my soul feel alive.

I felt free.

****

When I was 16 years old and I ran away from home my eldest sister said to me 'You know what Juliet. I think you're really brave for running away from home... but I'd say you're more stupid brave!'

Being 'Stupid Brave' has definitely been a strategy for me throughout my life.

And I firmly believe that the universe always rewards courage.

Even if it doesn't make logical sense.

If you wait until everything is perfect and aligned you will be waiting forever.

You have to make brave decisions in your life.

Even if they seem 'stupid brave' to everyone else!

Your courage will be rewarded.

Sometimes we seek external input from people around us to help us make decisions when we feel afraid. But I know now that the best person to seek counsel from, is ourselves.

I've been to three psychics in my life in my quest for answers, all at times when I needed some direction or guidance. When I was lost and wanted someone else to fix my problems or guide my future for me.

What's interesting is that they all gave me different readings, and yet they all told me exactly what I needed to hear at that time.

The first psychic I went to was when I was still with my ex-husband. I was so nervous beforehand about what she was going to tell me. She started my reading and said 'yep you'll be with him forever!' very matter of fact,

She said 'you wouldn't still be with your husband all this time if you weren't going to stay together forever!'

She kept saying the word FOREVER really firmly.

My intuition skipped in my gut and said to me very clearly 'No...I won't! She's wrong!'

She told me exactly what I needed to hear to learn to trust my intuition.

The second psychic I went to see was when I was dating the man after I left my husband. She described the house we were going to buy by the beach with a white picket fence. She described our two children. It was all so perfect. Too perfect.

She told me I would stay in my career for a long time and life would be simple.

It felt wrong. It felt like something important was missing... again, now in hindsight, the reading was for a life that I realised I didn't want!

The third psychic was the one who led me to Paul and the life I am leading today.

Needless to say, I think she is an incredibly gifted psychic because she was accurate, but I actually believe all three of them were.

Why?

All three contributed to my journey and taught me different lessons along the way.

All three gave me the exact readings I needed at that particular time in my life.

The reason I don't go to psychics anymore is that I believe it is possible (and more empowering) to be your own psychic.

To create your own future and to decide the circumstances of your own life.

How?

Well, I've already explained some of the techniques in the preceding chapters.

Through a combination of visualisation and 'playing out scenarios' we can sense or intuit potential outcomes in our lives.

So often our imagination is used in a negative way, but through this process we can use it to our advantage and I practice this every single day!

When making decisions, when choosing a path forward, when deciding what I want to happen in my life.

The **'Be Your Own Psychic'** process is as follows:

UNDESIRED OUTCOME

1. Think of a situation where you are worried or unsure about the outcome.
2. What is the worst thing that could happen?
3. Play out the worst-case scenario in your head as much as possible.
4. Write down what you would learn if that happened.
5. Now, decide if you want to learn those things that way, or if you would prefer to learn those things your way.

If you learn those lessons your way you will protect yourself from the need for the universe to bring you that situation in order to evolve.

Remember, we are always receiving whatever helps us grow and evolve. This is a way of intercepting challenging life situations and turning the ball into your court.

For example, imagine that the worst thing that could happen is losing your job. Perhaps, over the next few months you become so dissatisfied with work that you take sick days and start slipping in your performance.

Then eventually that leads to performance management issues and being fired. This impacts your self-confidence and stops you being able to pursue your dreams.

You would have to learn to rebuild, to look after yourself and find a new job and overcome adversity.

NOW, decide if you would rather choose to rebuild, look after yourself and find (or design) a new job?

What steps would you need to take to do this, before you create the situation of losing your job to force you to do this?

DESIRED OUTCOME

1. Now think of a situation where you would LOVE a certain outcome.
2. What is the best thing that could happen?
3. Play out the scenario in as much detail as you can.
4. Write down what you would learn if that happened, and who you need to be to have this situation occur.
5. Now, decide what things you need to learn and what resources you need in order to ensure that outcome occurs. Is there anything standing in your way? If so, what is

it? Write it down and realise you have the capacity to change or prepare for this.

For example, the best possible outcome might be receiving a new opportunity that was quite unexpected that opens doors for you in ways you never imagined!

You meet powerful influencers and are rewarded for your efforts. You would learn to look after yourself and your brand, and study and learn to sharpen your skills. You would need to be magnetic and have good energy to attract such an opportunity.

You may realise that there is actually nothing standing in your way other than imagining this desired outcome and visualising it often!

Spend as much time as you can visualising what you want. Too often, we use our imagination to visualise all the things we don't want.

This is a poor use of our own psychic abilities.

On the other hand, ask yourself, 'what is currently preventing me from having this outcome?'

Perhaps you need to change your CV, or contact an old friend in an industry you are interested in, or go to an event.

You can change your future - nothing is set in stone.

The 'Be Your Own Psychic' technique takes practice, and is one of the activities I guide my guests through at my live events.

Books are wonderful, but there really is nothing like a live, transformative experience.

There is an overwhelming amount of information in the world these days (especially on the internet), yet a lack of embodiment, transformation and integration and that's what I provide at my live events.

Whilst I am a huge advocate of being brave and stepping forward fully, I am also a firm believer in the philosophy of testing things to see what works first and then jumping all in.

Because, sometimes the fear is actually useful — it's like a warning light, encouraging us to check our blind spots before we move.

It's crazy to think that if you make a big change that you're not going to encounter any obstacles! I think some people have seen my journey and think it was all easy — that is far from the case!

I was propelled into inconsistent income, the unknown, adjusting to no longer working in a workplace with friends and colleagues, and not working typical 9-5 hours. It was a big adjustment. What inspired me to succeed was the promise I made to myself never to work in an office ever again. That was motivation in itself!

I think the biggest adjustment of all was the lack of routine.

So, in order to address this lack, I created my own morning routine in the first two months of leaving my job. This ensured I would start my day off focused, inspired and strong. I spent one hour each morning in the following way and called it the 'Relaunch My Life Routine':

The Relaunch My Life Routine

30 minutes of movement

20 minutes of meditation

10 minutes of journaling or goal-setting

This easy to follow formula gave me a stable and clear focus and a basis to build my business upon from the beginning of each new day.

I even posted every day about it on social media for 60 days and my posts gave me momentum, encouragement and free advertising for my business!

On day 60 I ran a public 'Relaunch My Life Routine' and was interviewed by a local radio station for being the first person to run a meditation in our city center.

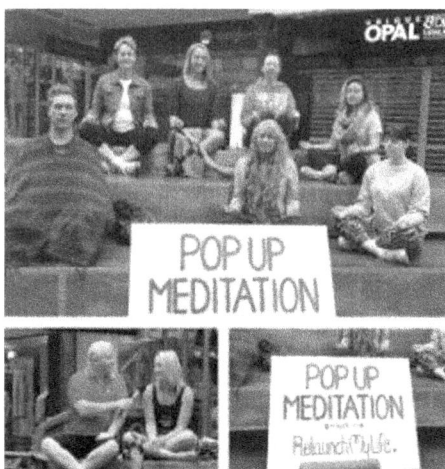

Image: Being interviewed by local Radio Station ABC Adelaide during my public Relaunch My Life routine.

In times of change, the more stability and routine you can provide yourself the more you will be able to handle the change.

No matter what you do in life you are going to have challenges. The challenges I have today are that I do not feel stuck and unfulfilled, the challenges are more around decisions and choices. My current challenge is to decide which publisher to go with and how to promote my book launch.

What I am trying to say is that there are still challenges and obstacles but they are different!

Preparation helps us overcome the illusion of fear and sometimes, you do need to leap before you feel ready, within reason.

Before I quit my job, I took the time to build my business on the side.

I spent months preparing. I spent months getting practice with clients (family and friends) and started building a reputation and getting momentum in my business before I took the leap. I had run a profitable one day workshop and gained momentum with my business.

I was connected to my soul and my intuition to 'sense' when it was time to leap. Self-doubt is normal when you are embarking on something new, but you never want fear to hold you back longer than it needs to.

Before I left my job I calculated my 'daily survival rate' so that I knew how much money I had and how much money I needed per day to survive. This knowledge brought me a great sense of relief.

This calculation is very empowering if you're thinking of quitting your job, or ending a relationship, or going overseas travelling, or doing something uncertain.

It takes you out of fear and grounds you practically which in turn helps you to feel safe with your decisions in life.

HOW TO CALCULATE YOUR DAILY SURVIVAL RATE

1. Add up all of your expenses into a monthly figure. Be sure to think of everything.

   Bills, housing costs, minimum repayments on credit cards or loans (as this is just about survival for the purpose of this exercise), food, business costs etc.

   Monthly Bills _____

2. Once you have this figure, multiply this number by 12 and divide it by 365. This gives you your daily survival rate.

    Daily Survival Rate _____

3. Now, to turn this dollar figure into something more tangible, the next step is to calculate how many days you can survive in your current situation.

    The way to do this is to add up all of your savings and cash that you have to your name. Ignore any debt owing for now (as you can pay these off once you start earning all your money).

    Total cash/savings _____

4. Now, divide your cash/savings figure above by your Daily Survival Rate.

    _____ days

This result shows you the number of days you can survive if you earn absolutely no income at all from today (which is unlikely to happen).

For example, if you had $4000 in savings, and your daily survival rate is $95 per day to survive. You would have 42 days to survive if you earned absolutely no income at all from today.

In the beginning of my business I calculated this number every single day. Even if you have lots of money it's a great exercise to complete.

The lowest I got to was 16 days. I felt safest when I could keep the number above 30.

Again, I walk you through this process at my live events, in my one on one coaching and at retreats.

Financial fear is a crippling fear, and one many women struggle with as a result of undervaluing ourselves.

These days I carry a $100 note in my purse with the words 'thank you for all the money I have ever received in my life' written on it as a simple visual reminder of the abundance that is always flowing to us in this world.

I also never place my handbag on the floor because I believe the floor is the lowest and least valuable place we can put our purse! Call me superstitious if you will, but it's a sign that I value my belongings and my finances.

Give it a try, for the next week, be conscious of where you place your handbag never letting it touch the floor.

Key take-aways

- The universe rewards courage.
- You can use the power of your own psychic abilities to predict future desired and undesired scenarios and make them happen differently, or prepare for them.
- Prepare first, but don't get addicted to preparation. Know when to step up and act.
- Calculate your daily survival rate to help you feel safe with your decisions.

Activities

- Use the 'Be Your own Psychic' process with as many scenarios (both good and bad) as possible this week.
- Practice the 'Relaunch My Life routine' one day this week.
- Calculate your Daily Survival Rate and keep an eye on how many days you can survive without receiving any income so you can stay relaxed about your situation.

A final word on fear:

When we let fear hold us back the whole world suffers. But most of all, when we hold our dreams back and commit to a life that doesn't light our soul up inside, we suffer.

The only thing worse than someone who has died, is someone whose body is still living even though their soul perished long ago.

The only thing worse than a relationship that has ended, is a relationship that exists on the surface when the love and commitment inside perished long ago.

And the only thing worse than an employee quitting or losing their job, is an employee who quit long ago, but still turns up to work every day simply to collect their pay cheque..

Make choices based on things that bring you joy, things that make you feel lighter and things that make you feel free.

Don't let your fears hold you back - let your heart send you forwards.

CHAPTER 11

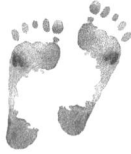

Take One Step Every Day

'Faith is taking the first step without seeing the entire staircase.'
– Martin Luther King Jr

Since I quit my job in 2014 and escaped the 9-5 rat race I have had an incredible journey.

People often tell me that I am inspiring and brave for setting up a business like this.

What they don't realise is I literally don't feel like I had a choice. I felt like the decision was bigger than me.

And a few years ago, my story is all I had.

So I built my business around my transformation and I became my own success story. But it's always just been one step at a time.

When I first started my business back in 2014, one day I registered my business name.

The next day I registered a website URL.

The next day I asked a friend to design me a logo.

Within a week my business was up and running.

One step at a time.

When I ran my first Bali retreat, I sold a ticket the day I found the perfect venue. Everything aligned and fell into place one step at a time.

When I decided to take the leap and teach personal development trainings and create new courses, people appeared out of nowhere saying how long they'd been waiting to do something like it.

Incredible things happen when we trust, when we are following our purpose and we take life one step at a time.

Keep your focus on the present whilst gently eyeing the horizon.

******

Finishing the last chapter of this book is just the next step for me. What is your next step?

In the first few months the hardest part was adjusting to being my own boss. At first, I was a terrible boss to myself! I was a slave driver... but then one day after feeling incredibly tired I realised, the greatest gift any of us can give the world is to be the happiest and most fulfilled version of ourselves. My marketing strategy is to reflect in my own life the happiness and fulfilment that my clients are seeking.

The balance of managing a self-created business is an interesting journey. It truly is a balancing act of managing my masculine planning and feminine receptive sides. Ensuring I am giving enough time to myself and nourishing my soul and enough time to my purpose, my relationship and my incredibly inspiring clients.

I ask myself daily 'how can I be of most service to this world?' I encourage you to ask yourself the same question as often as possible.

In preparing this book I calculated that I have so far supported over 1000 people through events, coaching and retreats to pursue their dreams and I know this number will continue to grow once I have this book out in the world.

Remember, the ripple effect of the brave decisions you make in your life will serve others. Remember the jigsaw puzzle of this planet - you fit someone else's part in serving this world. If you hold yourself and your magic back you hold everyone else back too.

In this chapter there are three things I want to leave with you to inspire you to live your most fulfilling life.

The first is to remember to **treat your life like a quest.**

Stay open and keep your eyes peeled for clues.

You may see the same person a few times, or hear a similar conversation, notice the patterns and clues in your life.

Don't ignore them!

The more clues you notice the more they can help you.

The second point is to **start having more fun.**

Your life is supposed to feel good to you!

Don't take it all so seriously, soon enough this game will be over and all the playing pieces will be back in the box.

Life goes quickly, and you only get to experience it now in this moment.

And finally, I want you to remember that all you need to do is **take your life, your purpose and your vision one step at a time.**

Years ago, if anyone had told me I would be running the business I have today - I simply wouldn't have believed them!

Trust that in each step you take you are going to grow, learn and change in ways that unravel your doubts, fears and insecurities.

You deserve to live your happiest and most fulfilling life.

So start saying yes to adventure, to variety, to uncertainty, to life changing experiences.

Say yes to it all!

The person you will be in a few years' time will be capable of things entirely different to what's possible for you to even comprehend right now.

You will meet people, have experiences and learn new things that shape your dreams and allow you to keep following your heart.

It's important to continually reconnect to yourself and what your soul desires as you change and grow, redesign your future based on your new abilities and rediscover the magic of who you truly are along the way.

This is not a once off process, these three steps are the key to an ongoing fulfilling life.

So, allow your vision to change, because as you change and grow your vision can too. If you get too fixed on one particular outcome, you could miss something truly magical.

Remember, all you need to do is take it one step at a time.

I can promise you, I never, ever, ever dreamed of writing a book when I first started out on this path a few years ago!

But now, it just feels like the logical next step.

One step at a time - that's all I ever take.

Perhaps you've been taking a step on the '30 days to Relaunch My Life' calendar to start off with?

This is a great way to gain momentum and realise that it is possible to focus on one thing every day.

Because, if you took one step towards your dreams every single day, that would be 365 steps per year.

And within 3 years you would have taken 1,000 steps towards your dreams!

This is pretty amazing to consider. The time will pass anyway. You may as well make the most of it!

On the other hand, your other choice is to do nothing differently and allow fear and uncertainty to direct your life.

And then, in 3 years time, you would have taken ZERO steps towards your dreams.

Zero versus 1,000 …

I know what choice I'd make.

As said by Sean Patrick Flanery - Do something today that your future self will thank you for!

Remember, no matter what your current reality is you can take one step every single day towards your dream life.

You deserve to live your happiest and most fulfilling life.

If I can change my life (and the lives of hundreds of women's lives) this dramatically in just a few short years, then I know it's possible that you can too.

In this book, you have a variety of tools to empower you to follow and trust your intuition, your wisest teacher.

Your path is going to be different to mine, but I trust that my story has ignited a spark within you to start making decisions for you and what makes you happy. And my story is really only just beginning!

Your definition of success today may be very different to mine, or even what it used to be.

And every decision you make is either taking you towards or away from your most fulfilling and authentic life.

TAKE-AWAYS

- See your life as a quest
- Start having more fun
- Remember, you only need to take one step at a time towards your dreams.

ACTIVITY

Take some time now to write the three biggest light-bulb moments you have had from reading this book:

1. _____

2. _____

3. _____

And share this step in the Facebook group 'Relaunch My Life Community'.

CHAPTER 12

Choose Your Own Adventure

This is where my story ends and **your story begins!**

What you do with this knowledge and journey is *entirely up to you.*

If you haven't already, join the Facebook Group 'Relaunch My Life Community'.

Visit www.julietlever.com to download your FREE resources and find out more about my courses and trainings.

So, what is your first and next step towards your dreams?

It could be something as simple as contacting someone you think can help you with an idea.

It could be researching courses to study and learn more about a particular topic.

It could be signing up for a local meditation, movement or yoga class.

Decide what your one next step is going to be after reading this book and write it here:

_____

_____

And please, share this step in the Facebook group 'Relaunch My Life Community'.

Remember, no one else knows what makes your soul feel alive but you!

So choose your own adventure.

And take one step towards your dreams every day.

Xx
With love and respect,
Juliet Lever

Notes:

_____

_____

_____

_____

_____

_____

_____

_____

_____

_____

_____

_____

_____

_____

Resources and References

Hindu Stages of Life
  http://www.hindunet.org/quickintro/hindudharma/hind
  u_four_stages.htm

Reiki Statistics:
  http://www.centerforreikiresearch.org/

Psychology Today Article:
  https://www.psychologytoday.com/blog/flourish/20091
  2/seeing-is-believing-the-power-visualization

Importance of Rituals
  http://www.huffingtonpost.com/donna-
  henes/rituals_b_3294412.html

Decision fatigue
  http://www.nytimes.com/2011/08/21/magazine/do-
  you-suffer-from-decision-fatigue.html

Women taking a year to decide what to wear
  http://www.telegraph.co.uk/news/uknews/5783991/Wo
  men-spend-nearly-one-year-deciding-what-to-
  wear.html

Leading Edge Journal Statistics on Decision Numbers
http://go.roberts.edu/leadingedge/the-great-choices-
of-strategic-leaders

Chakras
http://www.areconnecting.com/throat-
chakra.html#.WPQykFOGNE4

http://chakraenergy.com/intro.html

RECOMMENDED READING:

Braden, G. (2008). *The spontaneous healing of belief*. 1st ed. Carlsbad, Calif.: Hay House.

Coelho, P. (n.d.). *Alchemist, The*. 1st ed.

Coelho, P. and Costa, M. (1998). *Veronika decides to die*. 1st ed. London: HarperCollins.

Demartini, J. (n.d.). *The values factor*. 1st ed.

Hay, L. (2008). *You can heal your life*. 1st ed. Australia: Hay House.

Abraham, Hicks, E. and Hicks, J. (2007). *The astonishing power of emotions*. 1st ed. Carlsbad, Calif.: Hay House.

Lipton, B. (n.d.). *The biology of belief*. 1st ed.

Noontil, A. (1988). *The body is the barometer of the soul so be your own doctor*. 1st ed. Nunawading, Vic.: Annette Noontil.

Penczak, C. (2004). *Magick of Reiki*. 1st ed. St. Paul, Minn.: Llewellyn Publications.

Simpson, L. and Hale, T. (n.d.). *The book of chakra healing*. 1st ed.

QUOTES

Anaïs Nin and Ralph Waldo Emerson
http://www.positivityblog.com/index.php/2014/03/19/self-esteem-quotes/

Christiane Northrup
https://www.goodreads.com/work/quotes/41718350-goddesses-never-age-the-secret-prescription-for-radiance-vitality-and

Gregg Braden
http://www.azquotes.com/quote/633193

Ho'oponopono Prayer
http://consciouslifenews.com/heal-heart-relationships-hooponopono/1166691/#

Osho
http://peacefulrivers.homestead.com/Osho2.html

http://www.awakening-intuition.com/osho-quotes.html

Paolo Coehlo
https://www.goodreads.com/work/quotes/3287043-veronika-decide-morrer

https://quotecatalog.com/u/heidipriebe/2016/05/x-paulo-coelho-quotes-that-will-soothe-your-aching-heart

http://www.goodreads.com/quotes/7022248-do-something-today-that-your-future-self-will-thank-you

About the Author

Juliet Lever, is an Australian based Trainer, Author and Speaker who believes we all have the ability to redesign any element of our lives and live to our highest potential.

She personally redesigned her own life from being a stressed out workaholic, alcoholic, shopaholic in a passionless marriage to now living a life of her own design.

She has studied a Bachelor of Metaphysics with the University of Sedona, is a Certified Yoga Teacher, a Licensed Heartmath™ Resiliency Coach, a Reiki and Seichim Master, a Trainer of NLP and Time Line Therapy® techniques and Hypnosis Practitioner and also holds business qualifications in a Diploma of Business, Diploma of Neuro Psycho Immunology and Diploma of Finance Broking.

Juliet combines a practical corporate background with spiritual teachings to help humans dig deep into their hearts to find what makes their souls come alive.

Juliet lives in in South Australia with her soul-mate Paul and their dog Max and cat Sunny. Her second book 'Author Rising' is a guide to help you stop procrastinating and write your very own book.

Juliet personally responds to all email enquiries and would be honoured to hear from you wherever you are on your journey.

For enquiries you can visit her website
www.julietlever.com or email Juliet at
juliet@relaunchmylife.com.au